TOLERANCE, AUTOIMMUNITY
AND AGING

Publication Number 820

AMERICAN LECTURE SERIES[R]

A *Monograph* in

The BANNERSTONE DIVISION of
AMERICAN LECTURES IN GERIATRICS

Edited by

LEO GITMAN, M.D., F.A.C.P.

Chief, Gerontology Section, and Endocrine Clinics
The Brookdale Hospital Center
Brooklyn, New York

MARION E. BUNCH

Department of Psychology
Washington University
St. Louis, Missouri

MORRIS ROCKSTEIN, PhD.

Department of Physiology
University of Miami School of Medicine
Miami, Florida

TOLERANCE, AUTOIMMUNITY AND AGING

Compiled and Edited by

M. MICHAEL SIGEL, Ph.D.

Professor of Microbiology
University of Miami School of Medicine

and

ROBERT A. GOOD, M.D., Ph.D.

American Legion Memorial Research Professor
Regents' Professor of Pediatrics, Microbiology and Pathology
Head, Department of Pathology

With an Introduction by

Morris Rockstein, Ph.D.

Professor of Physiology and Radiology
Director, Training Program in Cellular Aging
University of Miami School of Medicine

CHARLES C THOMAS • PUBLISHER
Springfield · Illinois · U.S.A.

Published and Distributed Throughout the World by
CHARLES C THOMAS · PUBLISHER
BANNERSTONE HOUSE
301-327 East Lawrence Avenue, Springfield, Illinois, U.S.A.
NATCHEZ PLANTATION HOUSE
735 North Atlantic Boulevard, Fort Lauderdale, Florida, U.S.A.

© *1972, by* CHARLES C THOMAS · PUBLISHER
ISBN 0-398-02413-8
Library of Congress Catalog Card Number: 79-157295

With THOMAS BOOKS *careful attention is given to all details of manufacturing and design. It is the Publisher's desire to present books that are satisfactory as to their physical qualities and artistic possibilities and appropriate for their particular use.* THOMAS BOOKS *will be true to those laws of quality that assure a good name and good will.*

Printed in the United States of America
Y-2

CONTRIBUTORS

J. Werner Braun, Ph.D.
Rutgers, The State University
New Brunswick, New Jersey

Monroe D. Eaton, M.D.
Harvard Medical School
Boston, Massachusetts

John E. Hotchin, M.D., Ph.D.
New York State Department of Health
Albany, New York

Takashi Makinodan, Ph.D.
Oak Ridge National Laboratory
Oak Ridge, Tennessee

Henry Metzger, M.D.
National Institute of Arthritis and Metabolic Diseases
Bethesda, Maryland

Norman Talal, M.D.
National Institute of Arthritics and Metabolic Diseases
Bethesda, Maryland

Perry O. Teague, Ph.D.
College of Medicine
University of Florida
Gainesville, Florida

Morris N. Teller, Ph.D.
Sloan-Kettering Institute for Cancer Research
Rye, New York

Edmond J. Yunis, M.D.
University of Minnesota Hospital
Minneapolis, Minnesota

INTRODUCTION

A N APT corollary to Descartes's "cogito, ergo sum" might well be "cogito ergo scio me senectarum et moriturum esse" — that is to say, man as a thinking being is not only aware of his own existence, but of the fact that he, like all animals, must grow old and eventually depart his "mortal coil." Tremendous increase and interest on the part of competent scientists, representing various areas of the basic sciences in the universal biological phenomenon of aging, has led to serious as well as idle speculation as to the underlying causes of aging. Consequently, this has resulted in the proposal of a number of theories of aging, each too narrow to explain all facets of the total aging process in humans. Nevertheless, the phenomenon of aging, as an increasing inability to withstand the environmental impacts with advancing age, is being more and more accepted as a programmed event in the life of all complex animals, both as regards duration and direction.

With this continued involvement of more and more sound, basic scientists seeking new horizons, the generic science of gerontology has left its infancy, particularly in the past decade, and entered a period of growth and maturation. The establishment of the National Institute of Child Health and Human Development in 1963 has helped in the direction of focusing, through the Adult Development and Aging Branch of that Institute, intramural as well as extramural attention on both intensifying and broadening research efforts in the field of biological gerontology, and on attracting individuals with various scientific expertise into the field of aging research, by establishing training programs in selected institutions all over the country.

The Training Program in Cellular Aging at the University of Miami, supported by funds from the NICHD includes, as part of its formal instructional activities, an advanced seminar program.

The two-day symposium on "Tolerance, Autoimmunity and Aging," held in Miami on February 9-10, 1970, brought together a group of outstanding experts to discuss their respective research interests, especially as regards the involvement of autoimmune and immunological mechanisms in the aging process. This book is the edited summary of the proceedings of that symposium. The timeliness of this publication is evidenced by the publication, by Walford, of a monograph, *The Immunological Theory of Aging*, some time following the particular symposium in question.

To Drs. M. Michael Sigel and Robert A. Good must go the major credit for making possible the program itself and therefore the final publication of this work. To the participants in this Symposium, whose contributions thereto are included in this work, go my thanks especially for their cooperativeness in all dimensions. To Mrs. Edith Salmon, Administrative Secretary of this Training Program, goes my sincerest expression of appreciation for her complete involvement and dedication from its inception, in the many technical details of arrangements for the symposium which resulted in this work. Finally, I should like to acknowledge formally the support of the National Institute of Child Health and Human Development, for making possible in part (under Training Grant No. HD 00142) this important Symposium, as well as the enthusiastic interest of Mr. Payne E. L. Thomas, of Charles C Thomas, Publisher, in undertaking the publication of this significant contribution in the field of biological gerontology.

MORRIS ROCKSTEIN

CONTENTS

TOLERANCE, AUTOIMMUNITY AND AGING

Chapter 1

AGE-RELATED CHANGES IN ANTIBODY-FORMING CAPACITY *

TAKASHI MAKINODAN

INTRODUCTION

A N UNDERSTANDING of aging of the immune system requires a comprehensive quantitative study not only of individuals after adulthood, but also of individuals from birth to death. The reasons are twofold. One is that, as with some of the other complex systems, aging of the immune system may begin during maturation of the individual. The second is that studies limited to the aged may not permit one to determine to what extent changes in the immune system reflect intrinsic changes in the immunocompetent cell population and extrinsic changes in the environment (e.g., nutrient pool, regulatory factors, lymphoid tissue architecture).

In spite of their obvious clinical importance, comprehensive studies of age-related changes in the immune system have been very few. Most age-related studies have been limited to only a fraction of an individual's lifespan, specifically to the period of growth,[23, 27, 34] and what little data we have on the aged has been derived from clinical and epidemiological studies involving a multitude of variables.[23, 34] Nevertheless, we have made enough headway to conclude that the immune system ages in general and that aging is due to changes in both the intrinsic and extrinsic factors. This presentation will center around findings supporting this conclusion and those concerning the nature of these age-related changes. Because more detailed, quantitative studies have been based on the

*Research sponsored by the United States Atomic Energy Commission under contract with the Union Carbide Corporation.

3

response of effector cells synthesizing antibodies than on the response of effector cells involved in cellular immunity, our emphasis will be placed on the former.

GROWTH AND MATURATION

Although the time of earliest ability to synthesize antibody varies with the test antigen and the species, there is in general a marked increase in the ability to synthesize antibody during neonatal and juvenile life.[27] During these periods the growth of the immunocompetent cell population is much faster than that of the individual or the organs in which these cells reside. Thus, during the first month of life in mice, the doubling time of body weight and spleen mass is about fourteen days,[16,18,19] whereas the doubling time of the ability to synthesize antibody is about four days.[3,16,17,35] This means that in contrast to only about a fourfold increase in body and spleen weights during the first thirty days after birth, the immunologic capacity of mice, as measured by ability to synthesize antibody, increases over one hundredfold.

In addition to synthesizing only a meager amount of antibody, neonates are immature in their capacity to synthesize a variety of immunoglobulin antibodies, being limited primarily to synthesis of 19 S macroglobulin antibodies.[25,27] The adults, in contrast, synthesize a wide spectrum of 7 S immunoglobulin antibodies (immunoglobulin A, G, etc.), in addition to 19 S macroglobulin antibodies.

Inadequacy in the neonates' ability to synthesize antibody could be the result of a deficiency in either the immunocompetent cell population or the environment, or both. These possibilities can be easily tested by the cell transfer assay (Fig. 1-1).[14] Known numbers of dispersed lymphoid cells of neonates and adults, together with an optimum concentration of antigen, are infused into genetically compatible (syngeneic or isologous) adult and neonatal recipients. Because of prior exposure to x-radiation, the recipients are immunologically inert at the time of infusion. Their responses are then assayed serologically or in terms of the number of antibody-forming cells in a major lymphoid organ, such as the spleen. If the deficiency is in the immunocompetent cell population, the immunologic response of neonatal recipients of adult cells should be high, and the response of adult recipients of neonatal cells low. If,

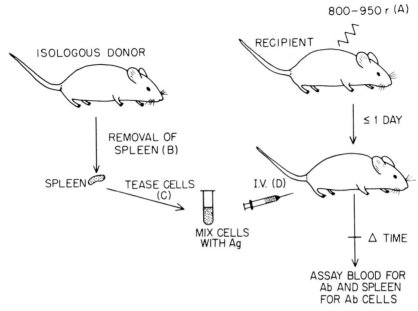

Figure 1-1. Schematic representation of the cell transfer method for cytokinetic studies of the immune response. After Makinodan *et al.*[14]

on the other hand, the deficiency is in the environment, the immunologic response of neonatal recipients of adult cells should be low, and the response of adult recipients of neonatal cells, high. The immunologic response of both neonatal recipients of adult cells and adult recipients of neonatal cells should be low if the deficiency is due to both factors. Studies of this type have revealed that deficiencies in both factors are responsible for the immunologic deficiency of the neonates.[1, 7, 8, 15-17, 26, 32]

The nature of these deficiencies has not yet been clearly elucidated, since studies in this area have been limited. The most comprehensive study is that of Bosma *et al.*[3] who were concerned with the nature of postnatal growth of the ability to synthesize antibody and the influence of naturally occurring microbial stimuli and maternal antibodies on this growth. Germ-free and conventional mice were used in this study, and dose-response and limiting-dilution assays were performed with their spleen cells. Bosma and co-workers found that there was a twelvefold increase in the ability to synthesize antibody between one and three months of age and that only about 25 percent of this growth can be accounted for by an increase in the number of immunocompetent units.* This would suggest that much of the difference between one-month and three-month-old mice in ability to synthesize antibody is due to a difference in the differentiation process of antigen-triggered immunocompetent units, i.e. a difference in the number of progenies generated per antigen-triggered immunocompetent unit and/or properties of the progeny (lifespan, quality of antibody synthesized, rate of synthesis, and secretion of antibody, etc.). They also found that neonatal and juvenile germ-free mice could not be distinguished from their conventional counterparts in terms of the rate and magnitude of increase in their immunologic capabilities. These results show that microbial flora and maternal antibodies have little influence on the growth and maturation of the immune system.

SENESCENCE

An indication that the immune system may undergo senescence as early as adolescence came from early studies on the age-related changes in serum natural antibody titers in man. Thomsen and Kettel[31] reported that among Europeans, serum A and B isoagglutinin titers rise rapidly to a peak level at about ten years of age and then decline gradually with advancing age, such that among individuals in their late sixties the titer is down to 25 percent of the peak level. Friedberger *et al.*[9] noted that the peak serum titer levels of naturally occurring heteroantibodies also occur at about ten years of age and decline gradually thereafter.

Studies on factors responsible for the occurrence of natural antibodies, especially in germ-free animals, indicate that they result from stimulation by antigens occurring naturally in the environment.[27] This would mean that changes in the immunologic activity of individuals may be primarily responsible for the age-related changes in natural antibody titers. Unfortunately, it was not until the past decade that comprehensive studies of senescence of the immune system were carried out.[6, 12, 15-18, 20, 28-30, 35] Most of these utilized mice of various strains and hybrids and of varying lifespans,

---

*An immunocompetent unit is a functional precursor unit of antibody-forming cells. The current view is that it is made up of a cluster of two to three cell types, of which one is the precursor cell that undergoes proliferation and differentiation into antibody-forming cells upon stimulation with an antigen.

and in general, the results were surprisingly similar to those based on natural antibody titers in man.[9, 31] It was found that the immunologic activity, as judged by the ability to synthesize antibody, increases rapidly to a peak level during the first few months of life and then begins to decline gradually. Typical age-related changes in the immunologic activity of conventionally reared mice, ranging in age from 4 to 124 weeks, are shown in Figure 1-2.[17] Also shown are changes in activity for the spleens of such mice, as assessed in

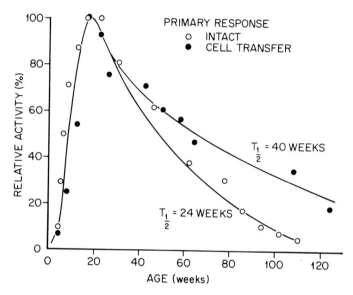

Figure 1-2. Relative primary antibody-forming activity of $BC3F_1$ mice and their spleens as a function of age (mean life span, 120 weeks). The spleen's activity was assessed by the cell transfer method. Maximum response of 100 percent is equivalent to the highest observed mean peak log_2 serum rat RBC agglutinin titer in each group, adjusted for age-dependent blood volume change in the case of intact mice. After Makinodan and Peterson.[17]

irradiated, syngeneic twelve-week-old recipients. We chose irradiated, young adult recipients because our previous studies[14] showed that the antibody-forming activity of spleen cells is maximally expressed in these animals. It can be seen that the age-related changes in the immunologic activity of intact mice were almost identical to those of the implanted spleens. The rate and magnitude of increase in immunologic activity between four and sixteen weeks of age was the same in both cases, as was the peak level of activity between sixteen and twenty weeks. This would indicate that the inadequacy in the immunologic activity between four and sixteen weeks of age reflects to a great extent, a deficiency in the immunocompetent cell population.

In both the intact animal and the implanted spleen, immunologic activity decreased gradually after twenty weeks of age, but the rates of decrease were different; i.e. the activity of the intact mice decreased much faster, with a halftime of about twenty-four weeks, in contrast to a halftime of about forty weeks for the spleens that were assayed in young adult recipients. The faster decay rate of the immunologic activity of the intact animal suggested to us that decrease in the activity of the immune system of aging mice is due not only to decrease in the activity of the immuno-

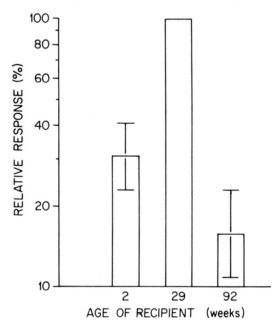

Figure 1-3. Relative primary antibody response of 10^8 spleen cells from twenty-nine-week-old BC3F$_1$ donors in irradiated, syngeneic recipients of various ages. Spleen cells were transferred with 10^8 rat RBC; thirty to sixty mice per group; vertical bars indicate 95 percent confidence limits; statistical analysis based on analysis of $\log_2$ seven-day serum titers. After Albright and Makinodan.[1]

competent cell population, but also to an environmental change that is not conducive to maximum expression of immunocompetent cells. To test this view the activity of spleen cells from adult syngeneic donors was assessed in irradiated young and aged recipients.[1] As shown in Figure 1-3, the activity of adult spleen cells in aged recipients was about 15 percent that in adult recipients, and in neonatal recipients it was 30 percent that in the adults. Comparable results were obtained by Metcalf *et al.*,[20] who implanted whole spleens and thymuses of adults into aged recipients, and Celada[4] has shown that although the activity of spleen cells of young donors were comparable in unirradiated, young and aged recipients, it was significantly lower in irradiated, aged than in irradiated, young recipients (Fig. 1-4).

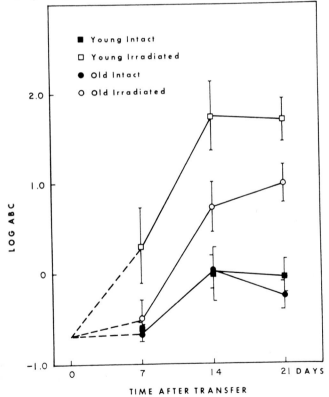

Figure 1-4. Antibody response profile of 2 x 10⁷ primed spleen cells after transfer with the test antigen (human serum albumin) into unirradiated and preirradiated syngeneic mice of two different ages. After Celada.[4]

As a model for the study of the role of extrinsic factors in growth and differentiation of immunocompetent cells, Perkins et al.[22] have been assessing the immunologic activity of spleen cells of young adult donors in irradiated, young adult, leukemia-prone AKR(H-2^k) and nonleukemia-prone C3H(H-2^k) recipients. Their preliminary studies revealed that, regardless of the type of donor cells, the activity was low in AKR and high in C3H (Fig. 1-5). This could have been the result of differences in donor-host histoincompatibility, but later studies failed to substantiate this notion.

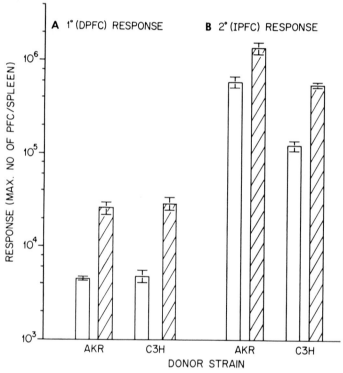

Figure 1-5. Strain difference in support of spleen cells undergoing primary (1°) and secondary (2°) responses. The responses were measured in terms of the maximum number of direct plaque-forming cells (DPFC) and indirect plaque-forming cells (IPFC) in the spleen of the recipient, after transfer of 5 x 10^7 nonprimed and 2.5 x 10^7 primed spleen cells with 10^9 sheep RBC into irradiated recipients. Vertical bars indicate one standard error; ten mice per group; recipient strain: □, AKR; ▨, C3H. After Perkins et al.[22]

In more recent work they obtained comparable results for hematopoietic spleen colony-forming cells and for spleen cells cultured in cell-impermeable diffusion chambers that were implanted into the peritoneal cavity. These results demonstrate that x-irradiated, leukemia-prone adult AKR mice do not support lymphohematopoiesis adequately because they either lack an essential humoral factor or release a factor that suppresses lymphohematopoietic cells. In

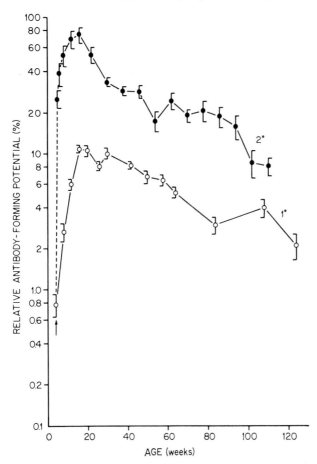

Figure 1-6. Relative primary and secondary antibody-forming activity of the spleen of BC3F$_1$ mice of varying ages. Maximum response of 100 percent taken as the highest observed individual peak titer. Vertical bars indicate one standard error; vertical arrow indicates time of primary immunization. After Makinodan and Peterson.[17]

contrast, x-irradiated, nonleukemia-prone strains of adult mice always maximally support lymphohematopoietic cells.

Age-related changes in secondary antibody-forming activity were determined by initially immunizing mice with an optimum dose of antigen when they were four weeks old and then assessing the activity of their spleens at various intervals thereafter.[17,18] The results (Fig. 1-6) showed that in immunized juvenile mice the peak activity of the spleen at sixteen to twenty weeks of age is tenfold greater than in nonimmunized mice. The secondary activity then decreases with a halftime of about ten months, a rate not significantly different from that of the nonimmunized mice. This suggests that, if mice are appropriately immunized only once during juvenility (i.e. at 4 weeks of age), their immunologic activity against the test antigen will always be greater than that of the unimmunized mice, even among the aged.

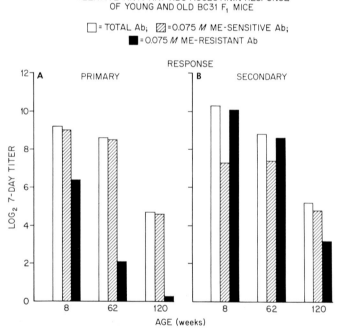

RELATIVE ANTI-RAT RBC AGGLUTININ RESPONSE
OF YOUNG AND OLD BC31 F_1 MICE

□ = TOTAL Ab; ▨ = 0.075 M ME-SENSITIVE Ab;
■ = 0.075 M ME-RESISTANT Ab

Figure 1-7. Relative peak mercaptoethanol (ME)-sensitive and -insensitive agglutinin responses against rat RBC of young and old BC3F$_1$ mice. After Makinodan and Peterson.[18]

Another study in progress concerns the immunizability of aged mice. Our preliminary data indicate that aged mice can be adequately immunized.[5] Thus, the secondary activity of aged mice four weeks after immunization appears to be only slightly lower than the primary activity of young mice.

In a study that needs to be extended because of its biologic implications, we assessed the quality (as judged by sensitivity to mercaptoethanol) of antibodies synthesized during the plateau phase of primary and secondary responses of 8-week, 62-week, and 120-week-old mice.[18] The results (Fig. 1-7) indicated that with advancing age the capacity to synthesize 7 S antibody is more severely affected than the capacity to synthesize 19 S antibody. In this respect aged mice are very similar to the neonates.

Other observations of interest concern the relationship between

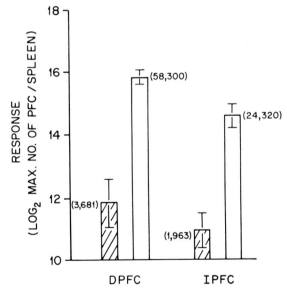

Figure 1-8. Comparison of peak antibody response of aged BC3F$_1$ mice with (A) follicle-invading reticulum cell sarcoma or (B) atrophy of the follicles of the spleen against aged BC3F$_1$ mice without A or B. ▨, mice with A or B; ☐, mice without A or B; DPFC, direct plaque-forming cells; IPFC, indirect plaque-forming cells; vertical bars indicate one standard deviation; mean number of PFC in parenthesis; twenty-one to fifty-nine samples per group; difference significant at the one percent level. After Chino and Makinodan.[5]

immunologic activity and pathology of aged mice. It should first be emphasized that reduced immunologic activity was detected even among mice without any lesions of the lymphatic tissue.[5, 11, 20] The activity of these mice was comparable to that of mice with nonneoplastic and neoplastic diseases, with two exceptions:[5] mice with atrophy of the spleen follicles and mice with reticulum cell sarcoma invading the spleen follicles. Figure 1-8 shows that the activity of the latter mice is less than ten percent of the others. Correlated with these findings is the observation of Legge and Austin, [13] who noted that antigens localized poorly in the follicles of aged mice.

Finally, Albright *et al.*[1, 2] performed a series of correlation studies that led to a dramatic alteration in the life expectancy of middle-aged BC3F₁ mice that normally have a long lifespan. It was first noted that with increase in age up to about 130 weeks there is an increasing likelihood that the spleen will enlarge,[16, 18] and with an increase in spleen size there is an increasing likelihood of lower immunologic activity and follicle-invasive reticulum cell sarcoma.[5]

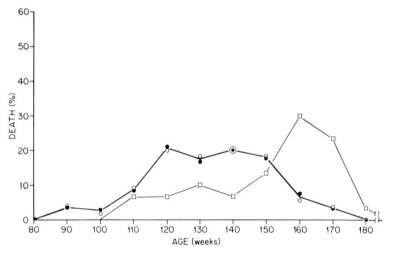

Figure 1-9. Distribution of death frequency at various ages of BC3F₁ mice as affected by splenectomy at ninety-seven weeks of age. ●, normal control (sample size, 96; ○, irradiated with 400 R at seventy-eight weeks of age and infused wth 10⁸ spleen cells from twelve-week-old donors (sample size, 55); □, splenectomized at ninety-seven weeks of age (sample size, 30). After Albright *et al.*[2]

Cell transfer studies revealed that transfer of spleen cells of aged (but not neonatal or adult) mice into irradiated, syngeneic, middle-aged (76-78 weeks old) recipients reduced the survival of the recipients. This life-shortening effect became progressively greater with increasing age of the donor mice (100-137 weeks). In contrast, splenectomy of mice at ninety-seven weeks of age extended their life expectancy. Thus, the median survival time of normal mice from age ninety-seven weeks was thirty-four weeks, whereas that of splenectomized mice was fifty-seven weeks (Fig. 1-9). Surgery of lymphoid organs in leukemia-prone strains of mice that have a relatively short lifespan produced similar results.[10, 21, 24, 33] These findings can explain why preliminary attempts at improving immunologic activity and extending life expectancy through transfer of lymphohematopoietic cells from juvenile donors have been unsuccessful:[1, 20] The transferred cells are unable to correct a pre-existing disturbance in the aged mice.

CONCLUSION

An attempt is made in this brief review to show that in general the activity of the immune system, as judged primarily by its capacity to synthesize antibody, increases exponentially during neonatal and juvenile life. It reaches its peak level during young adulthood and then decreases gradually, long before any currently known old-age-associated pathological diseases are manifested. The immunologic inadequacies of the neonates and the aged reflect both intrinsic deficiencies in the immunocompetent cell population and extrinsic deficiencies in the environment. The former are due to a decrease in the number of immunocompetent units and to a deficiency in the differentiation process of antigen-triggered precursors of antibody-forming cells. The latter include a humoral factor essential for the growth and differentiation of lymphohematopoietic cells, and factors which alter the architecture of the follicles.

Current studies on aging of the immune system are concerned not only with further clarification of extrinsic and intrinsic factors which are deficient especially in the aged, but also with the long-term effects of perturbation of the immune system. It is not surprising, therefore, that we are confronted with more questions now than we were a decade ago, when comprehensive studies in this area were initiated. Nevertheless, the outlook is most encouraging. Finally, mice have been used in most past studies of age-related problems in immunity because of their many advantages as test animals, but it is essential that other species be used, especially species that are distinct from the mouse both phylogenetically and metabolically.

REFERENCES

1. Albright, J.F., and Makinodan, T.: *J Cell Physiol, 67 (Suppl. 1)*:185-206, 1966.
2. Albright, J.F., Makinodan, T., and Deitchman, J.W.: *Exp Geron, 4*:267-276, 1969.
3. Bosma, M.J., Makinodan, T., and Walburg, H.E., Jr.: *J Immun, 99*:420-430, 1967.
4. Celada, F.: In Engel, A., and Larsson, T. (Eds.): *Cancer and Aging.* Stockholm, Nordiska Bokhandelns Förlag, 1968, pp. 97-108.
5. Chino, F., and Makinodan, T.: *Fed Proc, 29*:27, 1970 (Abstract).
6. Diener, E.: *Intern Arch Allerg, 30*:120-131, 1966.
7. Dixon, F.J., and Weigle, W.O.: *J Exp Med, 105*:75-83, 1957.
8. Dixon, F.J., and Weigle, W.O.: *J Exp Med, 110*:139-146, 1959.
9. Friedberger, E., Bock, G., and Fürstenheim, A.: *Z Immunitätsforsch, 64*:294-319, 1929.
10. Furth, J., and Boon, M.C.: In Moulton, F.R. (Ed.): *AAAS Research Conference on Cancer.* Washington, D.C., AAAS, 1945, pp. 129-138.
11. Hanna, M.G., Jr., Nettesheim, P., Ogden, L., and Makinodan, T.: *Proc Soc Exp Biol Med, 125*:882-886, 1967.
12. Kishimoto, S., Tsuyuguchi I., and Yamamura, Y.: *Clin Exp Immun, 5*:525-530, 1969.
13. Legge, J.S., and Austin, C.M.: *Aust J Exp Biol Med Sci, 46*:361-365, 1968.
14. Makinodan, T., Perkins, E.H., Shekarchi, I.C., and Gengozian, N.: In Holub, M., and Jaroskova, L. (Eds.): *Mechanisms of Antibody Formation.* Prague, Publishing House of Czechoslavakian Academy of Science, 1960, pp. 182-189.
15. Makinodan, T., and Peterson, W.J.: *Proc Nat Acad Sci USA 48*:234-238, 1962.
16. Makinodan, T., and Peterson, W.J.: *J Immun, 93*:886-896, 1964.
17. Makinodan, T., and Peterson, W.J.: *Develop Biol, 14*:96-111, 1966.
18. Makinodan, T., and Peterson, W.J.: *Develop Biol, 14*:112-129, 1966.
19. Metcalf, D.: In Good, R.A., and Gabrielson, E. (Eds.): *The Thymus in Immunobiology.* New York, Harper and Row, 1964, pp. 150-179.
20. Metcalf, D., Moulds, R., and Pike, B.: *Clin Exp Immun, 2*:109-120, 1967.
21. Nakakuki, K., Shisa, H., and Nishizuka, Y.: *Acta Haemat, 38*:317-323, 1967.

22. Perkins, E.H., Makinodan, T., and Upton, A.C.: *Fed Proc, 28*:499, 1969 (Abstract).
23. Ram, J.S.: *J Geron, 22*:92-107, 1967.
24. Siegler, R., and Rich, M.A.: *J Nat Cancer Inst, 38*:31-50, 1967.
25. Smith, R.T.: In Wolstenholme, G.E.W., and O'Connor, C.M. (Eds.): *Cellular Aspects of Immunity,* Ciba Foundation Symposium. Boston, Little, Brown and Co., 1959, pp. 348-368.
26. Sterzl, J.: *Folia Microbiol, 8*:69-79, 1963.
27. Sterzl, J., and Silverstein, A.M.: *Advances Immun, 6*:337-460, 1967.
28. Stjernsward, J.: *J Nat Cancer Inst, 37*:505-512, 1966.
29. Teller, M.N., Stohr, G., Curlett, W., Kubisek, M.L., and Curtis, D.: *J Nat Cancer Inst, 33*:649-656, 1964.
30. Teller, M.N., and Eilbert, M.: *J Nat Cancer Inst, 39*:231-239, 1967.
31. Thomsen, O., and Kettel, K., Z *Immunitätsforsch, 64*:67-93, 1929.
32. Trnka, Z., and Sterzl, J.: In Holub, M., and Jaroskova, L. (Eds.): *Mechanisms of Antibody Formation.* Prague, Publishing House of Czechoslavakian Academy of Science, 1960, pp. 190-194.
33. Upton, A.C.: In Wolstenholme, G.E.W., and O'Connor, M. (Eds.): *Carcinogenesis,* Ciba Foundation Symposium. 1959, pp. 249-268.
34. Walford, R.L.: *Advances Geron Res, 2*:159-204, 1967.
35. Wigzell, H., and Stjernsward, J.: *J. Nat Cancer Inst, 37*:513-517, 1966.

Chapter 2

INTERRELATIONSHIPS AMONG AGING, IMMUNITY AND CANCER*

INTRODUCTION

THE all-inclusive incidence of cancer seems intimately related to aging. Excluding childhood cancer, surveys taken in the United States in 1937-39 and 1947-48 show the following approximate incidences of cancer per 100,000 population: 40 at age twenty-five, increasing to 475 by age fifty, and to almost 2000 by age seventy-five.[1] A positive correlation clearly exists between the incidence of cancer and chronological age, but this does not indicate that cancer and physiological aging are necessarily directly related. Regardless, the prevalence of cancer among the aged is of increasing concern because of their steadily growing numbers.

It was believed that basic information elucidating the apparent association between cancer and aging might be obtained by a study of changes in homeostasis prior to and in the formative stages of a neoplasm. Immunity was the first homeostatic mechanism investigated.

RESULTS AND DISCUSSION

Initial explorations with random bred female Swiss mice revealed an impaired immune response, which increased directly with age. Other experiments using similar mice revealed a cumulative incidence of cancer that also increased with age. The first efforts directed to confirmation were followed by attempts to determine

*Supported in part by grants from the American Cancer Society, Inc., and the Milheim Foundation for Cancer Research; by contract SA-43-ph-2445 from the Cancer Chemotherapy National Service Center, and grants T4CA-5015 and CA 08748, National Cancer Institute, National Institutes of Health, Public Health Service.

18

what specific aspects of the immune mechanism were involved in this decrease in immune reactivity.[2-5]

Cancer Incidence

We observed a relatively high incidence of spontaneous tumors in the random bred Swiss mouse used for general experimentation. These tumors, which appeared in females about twelve months of age, occurred less frequently in males. The incidence of spontaneous tumors was, therefore, surveyed in three groups of mice: female and male breeders, and female virgins. At twenty-two months of age, it was 26 percent for female breeders, 21 percent for female virgins, and 7 percent for male breeders (Fig. 2-1). Although life spans differed, the final total tumor incidence was 26 percent for female breeders, 27 percent for female virgins, and 13 percent for male breeders.

Initial tumors occurred much later in males. There were a large number of types representing many organ sites. This was in contrast to the one or more predominant types peculiar to certain other strains of inbred mice.

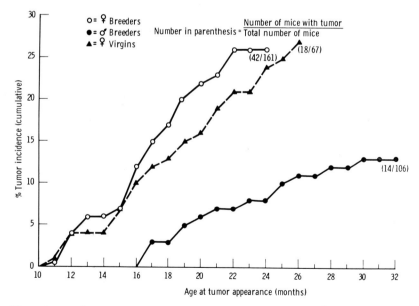

Figure 2-1. Cummulative spontaneous tumor incidence in ICR/Ha mice with respect to latency of appearance.

Tolerance, Autoimmunity and Aging
Homograft Response
Preliminary studies with a small series of female breeder Swiss mice revealed that a number of subcutaneous implants of the transplantable human tumor, H. Ep. #3 grew in those aged ten to fourteen months. Since this human tumor had not previously been seen to grow in untreated weanling or older mice or rats, it was transplanted into Swiss mice of various ages to determine whether its acceptance was related to the age of the host.

The human tumor graft grew, as expected, in almost 100 percent of the neonatal mice implanted when less than sixteen hours old (Fig. 2-2). In middle-aged and older mice the incidence of tumor takes was less frequent, but increased with the age of the mice. In females one to eight months old takes were negligible. Of the 462 mice implanted, small growths occurred in two eight months old and in one three months old. So that all mice six months of age and older would be similar, only those that had been bred one or more times were included in the series. Results revealed that the immune response of some mice was indeed impaired and that the percentage of those with impaired response increased with age.

Because of the strong potential of tumor cells for growth, another measurement of the homograft response was included: survi-

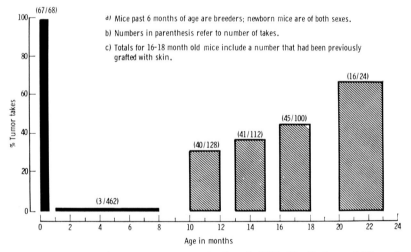

Figure 2-2. Takes of H. Ep. #3 tumor in female ICR/Ha Swiss and Taconic Swiss mice of various ages.

val of normal homologous skin grafts.

The graft procedure of Billingham and Medawar was used,[6] and young adult females served as donors of skin. The mean survival time of grafts on young adult females was 9.8 days, and on female breeders twelve to fifteen months old, 19.2 days (Table 2-I). The standard deviation for the old mice was very large because of the extended survival times of many grafts. The maximum survival was 15 days for young adult females and 252 days for old females. Although grafts survived longer on old than on young males, the difference was not statistically significant. Some of the grafts on old females were permanent. It was concluded, then, that the homograft reaction was the same for normal and transplanted tumor tissue.

TABLE 2-I

EFFECTS OF AGE AND SEX ON SKIN-GRAFT SURVIVAL
IN ICR/HA SWISS MICE

Donor Age (Mo)	Sex	Recipient Age (Mo)	Sex	Number Mice Grafted	Mean Survival Time (Days)	Maximum Mean Survival Time (Days)
2-3	♀	2-3	♀	128	9.8 ± 1.5*	15.0
2-3	♀	12–15	♀ B†	190	19.2 ± 32.3	252.0‡
2-3	♀	2	♂	25	9.5 ± 2.0	14.5
2-3	♀	12–14	♂ B	34	11.5 ± 2.6	17.5

*±Standard deviation.
†B, breeder.
‡Died with graft not rejected.

Reticuloendothelial System

Since the reticuloendothelial system is involved in immunity, its functional capacity in aging mice was measured: a) under normal conditions, b) during stimulation of the reticuloendothelial system, and c) during growth of an homologous tumor under both normal and stimulated conditions. The phagocytic index K was determined by the carbon clearance procedure of Biozzi *et al.*[7] Zymosan was the nonspecific stimulant for the reticuloendothelial system.

The phagocytic index K was greater in young adults than in middle-age or old mice (Fig. 2-3). The "corrected" phagocytic index, alpha, which takes into consideration the weights of liver and spleen where the greatest proportion of phagocytic activity occurs,[7] showed that the three-month and eight-month old mice had approximately the same rates of phagocytosis. However, that for old adults clearly differed.

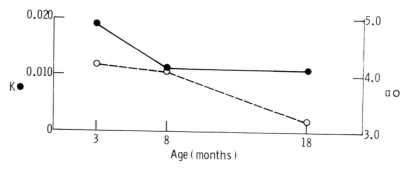

Figure 2-3. Phagocytic activity of normal ICR/Ha Swiss mice of various ages. Each *point* represents the mean of 10-15 mice. K = kinetic phagocytic index; a = corrected phagocytic index.

Zymosan stimulated phagocytic activity, caused the greatest increase in the young adults, and the least in the old animals (Fig. 2-4). The level of activity remained fairly high in the young mice, but decreased to almost normal in the old mice by the eighteenth day.

Groups of mice were pretreated with zymosan and inoculated seven days later with the homologous Ehrlich ascites tumor. The

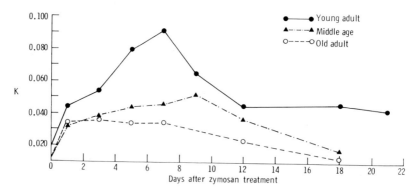

Figure 2-4. Variation in phagocytic activity of normal ♀ ICR/Ha Swiss mice after zymosan injection. Each *point* represents the average of five to six mice. K = kinetic phagocytic index.

tumor was rejected by six of the forty-one young adults, but by none of the middle-age or old mice (Table 2-II). Furthermore, as reflected in the mean survival times, the trend of tumor growth was faster in the old than in the young mice that were stimulated and nonstimulated. The latter were from the nonpretreated groups.

TABLE 2-II

TUMOR REJECTION AND SURVIVAL TIME OF ♀ SWISS MICE OF VARIOUS AGES AFTER INTRAPERITONEAL INOCULATION OF 5 × 10⁴ EHRLICH ASCITES TUMOR CELLS*

Age (Mo.)	Non-pretreated Survival Time (Days)‡	No. Rejections Total Number	Zymosan Pretreated† Survival Time (Days)	No. Rejections Total Number
3	15.1 ± 4.1	0/50	19.5 ± 6.0§	6/41
8	14.9 ± 4.9	0/20	14.6 ± 3.4	0/20
18	12.5 ± 3.5	0/22	14.7 ± 4.7	0/20

*5 × 10⁴ tumor cells injected intraperitoneally; survivors observed 2 mos.
†Zymosan (1 mg/gm body wt.) was injected intravenously 7 days prior to tumor transplantation.
‡Mean ± S.D.
§Excluding mice rejecting tumors.

Humoral Response

In continued experiments to clarify the factors involved in decreased immune reactivity accompanying aging, the capacity to form cytotoxic isoantibodies and antibodies with opsonic activity were measured. Mice in three age groups were tested for their ability to form cytotoxic antibodies against the strain specific C57Bl ascites leukemia, EL4. The immunization procedure consisted of one intradermal inoculation followed eight weeks later by an intraperitoneal inoculation of EL4 cells. The cytotoxic antibody test of Gorer and O'Gorman,[8] as modified by Boyse *et al.*,[9] was used.

Following the intradermal inoculation of 5×10⁴ cells, EL4 did not grow in any of the fifty young mice. However, twenty-seven of the forty-nine old mice died with progressively growing tumors. A second inoculation of 2×10⁶ cells was rejected by both young and surviving old mice. Blood samples were taken weekly, and the serum was pooled separately for each age group. Since progressive growth was not detected before the third week after the first inoculation, the sera from all old mice were pooled weekly for the first two weeks. Samples of the same sera from the various groups were used in the cytotoxic and opsonic activity procedures. The cytotoxic titer is defined here as the reciprocal of that dilution of immune serum in which the proportion of dead cells most nearly approximates 50 percent.

Three weeks after the first immunization, sera from young mice reached a maximum cytotoxic titer of about 16 (Table 2-III). The

TABLE 2-III

CYTOTOXIC ACTIVITY OF SERA FROM YOUNG AND OLD MICE
AFTER FIRST INOCULATION OF 5×10^5
LEUKEMIA CELLS INTRADERMALLY
(Aoki and Teller, 1966)

Group	Time After 1st Inoculation (Wk)	% Cells Stained by Trypan Blue Antiserum Dilution*						
		2	4	8	16	32	64	128
	1	26	27	30	26	<10		
	2	>95	>95	68	30	<10		
3-Mo Old	3	>95	94	68	63	<10		
Mice	4	88	>95	78	54	25	<10	
Rejecting	5	>95	>95	88	64	23	14	<10
EL4	6	>95	>95	79	56	44	11	<10
	7	60	>95	>95	80	24	<10	
	8	46	63	>95	87	13	<10	
	1	<10	<10	<10	<10			
	2	30	42	21	<10			
18-Mo-Old	3	55	45	22	18	13	<10	
Mice	4	37	58	27	20	<10		
Rejecting	5	33	50	47	24	14	<10	
EL4†	6	22	29	30	13	<10		
	7	14	14	<10	<10			
	8	<10	<10	<10	<10			
18-Mo-Old	3	22	12	<10	<10			
Mice With	4	14	14	14	<10			
Prog. Growing	5	23	23	13	<10			
EL4 Tumor‡	6§	18	19	15	<10			

*Reciprocal of dilutions.
†First and 2nd week sera represent pools from all old mice, including those in which progressive tumor growth was later determined.
‡All survivors were dead by end of 6th week.
§Serum pool from 4 mice.

activity persisted at this level through the eighth week. In old mice that rejected EL4 there was a lag of at least one week. The cytotoxic titer reached 4 by the fourth week, followed by a continuous decline after the fifth week. However, in old mice with progressively growing tumors, no fifty percent endpoint was reached.

The cytotoxic titer of sera obtained after the second inoculation of EL4 cells is shown in Table 2-IV. In young mice, the cytotoxic titer peaked immediately to 256 at the end of the first week, and thereafter declined gradually to between 16 and 32 at the end of the fourth week. However, the cytotoxic titer of sera from old mice reached from 16 to 32 at the end of the first week and decreased from 8 to 16 after two weeks; less than fifty percent of the cells were stained thereafter. Apparently, the second immunizing dose stimulated both young and old animals, but the decay of activity was more rapid in the old mice.

TABLE 2-IV

CYTOTOXIC ACTIVITY OF SERA FROM YOUNG AND OLD MICE
AFTER SECOND INOCULATION OF EL4 LEUKEMIA CELLS*

| *Time After 2nd Inoculation (Wk)* | | | | | *% Cells Stained. by Trypan Blue Antiserum Dilution†* | | | | | | |
Group		2	4	8	16	32	64	128	256	512	1024	2048
3-Mo-	1	>95	>95	>95	>95	>95	>95	76	51	44	25	<10
Old	2	83	>95	>95	>95	>95	>95	>95	30	18	<10	
Mice	3	84	83	>95	>95	>95	>95	38	24	22	<10	
	4	76	74	>95	77	38	16	<10				
18-Mo-	1	51	>95	>95	79	27	20	<10				
Old	2	>95	86	83	10	<10						
Mice	3	41	16	<10	<10							
	4	13	<10	<10	<10							

*2 X 10⁶ cells given i.p.
†Reciprocal of dilutions.

The test of Bennett[10] was used to quantitate the production of isoantibodies as specific opsonins for the phagocytosis of allogeneic tumor cells. Macrophages were obtained from peritoneal rinsings of young female Swiss mice injected three days earlier with starch suspensions. After the first immunizing dose, the opsonic activity of sera from young mice increased rapidly, reaching a maximum level of about 250 phagocytized EL4 tumor cells four weeks later (Fig. 2-5). This approximate level persisted for an additional four weeks. However, the opsonic activity of sera from old mice with tumor regression increased more gradually. It did not reach its peak of about 150 phagocytized tumor cells until six weeks post inoculation. The opsonic activity of sera from old mice with progressively growing tumors was low. After a three-week lag, the number of phagocytized EL4 cells increased gradually to a maximum of about eighty before the last four mice died after the sixth week. Figure 2-5 also shows that, following the second inoculation, the differences in the activities of sera from young and old mice remained the same.

To further clarify the association of aging and immunity with cancer, the immune reactivities of mice with high and low propen-

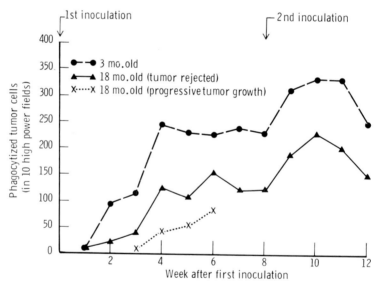

Figure 2-5. Opsonic activity of sera from young and old ♀ ICR/Ha mice after inoculation of EL4 leukemia cells. ● - - - ●, sera from young mice rejecting EL4; ▲———▲, sera from old mice rejecting EL4 (except for sera collected for Weeks 1 and 2, where all old mice contributed; x....x, sera from old mice developing progressive growth of EL4 tumor. First inoculation, 5x10⁵ cells, intradermally, on Day 0; 2nd inoculation, 2x10⁶ cells, i.p., on Day 56.

sities for spontaneous tumors were studied. Cytotoxic activity of immune sera of five inbred strains and one random bred line of Swiss mice with known incidences of spontaneous tumors[5] were investigated at various age levels. To avoid possible homologous tumor growth in the aged mice, irradiated tumor cells were used for immunization. Consequently, a rapid immunization procedure consisting of eight doses of irradiated cells in three weeks was devised to obtain a reasonable titer. A comparison of 50 percent endpoints as Log$_2$ titers is illustrated in Figure 2-6.

The cytotoxic titers were high or relatively high in sera from SJL and A/He mice up to at least twelve months of age, during

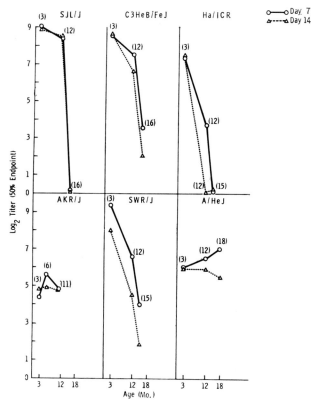

Figure 2-6. Cytotoxic antibody titers (log$_2$, 50 percent endpoint) of female mice of different strains and ages. Sera were collected on days 7 and 14 after the last immunizing dose of x-irradiated EL4 cells. Numbers in parentheses refer to age of the group in months.

which period these strains have high incidences of spontaneous tumors. Whereas a decrease in cytotoxic activity at advanced age occurred in four of the six strains tested, serum for A/He mice exhibited continuously increasing cytotoxic titers to eighteen months of age. During the life span of the AKR mice (none survived longer than 11 months), the titers remained at moderate levels.

Individual sera were also tested from nine AKR mice, a strain which exhibits leukemia in over 90 percent at an average of eight months. The titers were substantial both in the presence and in the absence of leukemia (Table 2-V). However, it must be noted that multiple immunizing doses were used; single doses might have produced different results. Table 2-VI illustrates the increase in titers brought about by a multiple dose schedule. In this experiment, hemagglutinin antibody against human erythrocytes was measured in sera from immunized mice three, eight and sixteen months old. Repeated weekly injections of the red blood cells caused such increases in titers that even sera from old mice contained relatively large amounts of antibody by the fifth week, despite an initial lag of about two weeks. Parenthetically, this situation, in which frequent doses of antigen are given, might be analogous to the situation in which a newly-arising neoplasm serves as a continuous source of antigen. The important assumption, certainly, is that such cells are antigenic very early. It is precisely at this time that

TABLE 2-V

CYTOTOXIC ANTIBODY TITERS (LOG$_2$, 50% ENDPOINT)
OF SIX-MONTH-OLD AKR/J ♀ BREEDERS
(Sera were collected one and two weeks after the last immunizing dose.)

Mouse No.	Week 1	Week 2	Diagnosis	
			Gross	Microscopic
1	5.6	5.7	Normal	No leukemia
3	4.0	3.9	Thymus enlarged	Incipient leukemia
4	6.4	6.5	Normal	Incipient leukemia
6	5.0	6.8	Normal	No leukemia
7	5.3	5.4	Large thymus and nodes	Leukemia
9	6.4	6.4	All organs enlarged	Leukemia
10	4.4	2.8	All organs enlarged	Leukemia
11	6.6	4.1	Thymus enlarged	Leukemia
12	5.5	3.5	All organs enlarged	Leukemia

TABLE 2-VI

HEMAGGLUTININ ANTIBODY TITERS IN FEMALE ICR/HA MICE
OF VARIOUS AGES, IMMUNIZED AT WEEKLY INTERVALS
WITH HUMAN ERYTHROCYTES

Age (*Mo.*)	*Average Titer Week*					
	0	1	2	3	4	5
3[9]	<2	16	64	256	512	2048
8[5]	0	8	16	128	256	1024
16[5]	0	<2	4	32	256[4]	512[4]

(Number in parenthesis refers to number of mice tested.)
(Test carried out by Dr. G. I. Avdeyev)

a lag in response or a weak response becomes of great importance in the progression of the disease.

These data, then, have revealed that: compared with young adult mice, aged female mice a) were less capable of rejecting skin homografts and tumor homografts and heterografts; b) had a decreased phagocytic activity of the reticuloendothelial system, and c) produced relatively low titers of isoantibody. Both cellular and humoral responses were impaired in these aged female mice.

It was also found that spontaneous tumor incidence increased cumulatively with age. It follows, then, that in such hosts, when an immune response is called for by an antigen, which per se can vary in strength, four questions arise: a) *Does* the response take place? b) If so, *how soon* does it occur? c) What is the *magnitude* of the response? d) What is the *duration* of the response? If it is assumed that host immunity is important in the initial stages of neoplasia, as well as in the progresssion of the disease, then a critical situation can exist during aging.

Immunodepression and Cancer

The data generally support the hypothesis that aging may be accompanied by an impaired immune reactivity which may increase susceptibility to cancer induction or release a neoplasm from control. There is additional tangential evidence that a close association exists between immunity and neoplasia. This is provided by reports of increased tumor incidence and decreased latency in animals in which immunological responsiveness has been depressed surgically, biologically, or chemically. A few examples follow.

Thymectomy in the neonatal period or early in life often decreases immunologic capacities in a number of species, as shown by Miller[11] in mice, Good et al.[12] in mice, and rabbits and Waksman et al.[13] in rats. Stjernswärd[14] reviewed briefly the enhancement of tumor induction by viruses and chemical oncogens following the use of this technique. With respect to biologic agents, Salaman[15] reported that oncogenic viruses have immunodepressive activity. Of interest too is a paper by Malakian and Schwab.[16] They showed that a cytoplasmic component of Group A streptococci suppresses both 19S and 7S antibody responses of mice to sheep erythrocytes. Such activity by bacterial products may have serious implications since this microorganism is a common contaminant in our environment. In the case of chemical carcinogens, Malmgren et al.[17] reported that compounds known to be oncogenic depress antisheep hemolysin antibody titers in mice and that this is not caused by their noncarcinogenic analogs. Rubin[18] and Prehn[19] showed that mice treated with methylcholanthrene had a diminished capacity to reject homografts. After a single exposure to methylcholanthrene, Stjernswärd[14] found that in mice the number of plaque-forming spleen cells was depressed for a long period which, in fact, corresponded to the latency of tumor development. In addition, there was a specific decrease in plaque-forming cells within the nucleated spleen cell population after host exposure to benz(a)pyrene, 7, 12-dimethylbenz(a)-anthracene or methylcholanthrene, but not to several noncarcinogenic hydrocarbons. Also relative to immunity and carcinogenesis, Stutman[20] reported that methylcholanthrene depressed the number of spleen plaque-forming cells in C_3Hf/Bi mice, a strain susceptible to the oncogenic effect of methylcholanthrene, but that it had no effect in strain I mice, which are relatively resistant to this carcinogen.

Preliminary results from our laboratory confirm the effectiveness of hormonal immunosuppression on tumor incidence and latency.

Brown et al.[21] and Teller et al.[22] reported that several analogs of purine, especially 3-hydroxyxanthine and guanine 3-oxide, are highly oncogenic. Rats were injected with 3-hydroxyxanthine at a dose that provides an approximate 50 percent tumor incidence at eighteen months after the first of eight weekly doses. Neonatal thymectomy did not alter tumor incidence significantly. However, when intact rats were given the carcinogen plus cortisone, a 50 percent tumor incidence occurred by seven months and ninety percent by ten months. As yet, the status of the purine-N-oxides as immunodepressants is unknown.

Finally, in the experimental system used, the data presented here establish a relationship between aging and spontaneous tumor incidence, and between aging and impaired immune response. The results of two attempts to determine whether spontaneous tumor incidence and depressed immunity are directly related were not successful (unpublished results). Continuous treatment with 6-mercaptopurine or corticosterone, 2 immunosuppressants, led to high mortality from toxicity and infection. The evidence for a direct effect of depressed immunity on spontaneous tumor incidence remains only suggestive.

REFERENCES

1. Dorn, H.F., and Cutler, S.J.: Morbidity from cancer in the United States. *Public Health Monogr*, no. 56, United States Department of Health, Education and Welfare, 1959.
2. Teller, M.N., Stohr, G., Curlett, W., Kubisek, M.L., and Curtis, D.: Aging and cancerigenesis. I. Immunity to tumor and skin grafts. *J Nat Cancer Inst, 33*:649-656, 1964.
3. Aoki, T., Teller, M.N., and Robitaille, M.L.: Aging and cancerigenesis. II. Effect of age on phagocytic activity of the reticuloendothelial system and on tumor growth. *J Nat Cancer Inst, 34*:255-264, 1965.
4. Aoki, T., and Teller, M.N.: Aging and cancerigenesis. III. Effect of age on isoantibody formation. *Cancer Res, 26*:1648-1652, 1966.
5. Teller, M.N., and Eilbert, M.: Aging and cancerigenesis. IV. Interrelationships among age, immune response and tumor incidence in several strains of mice. *J Nat Cancer Inst, 39*:231-239, 1967.
6. Billingham, R.F., and Medawar, P.B.: The techniques of free skin-grafting in mammals. *J Exp Biol, 28*:385-402, 1951.
7. Biozzi, G., Benacerraf, B., and Halpern, B.N.: Quantitative study of the granulopectic activity of the reticuloendothelial system. *Brit J Exp Path, 34*:441-457, 1953.
8. Gorer, P.A., and O'Gorman, P.: The cytotoxic activity of isoantibodies in mice. *Transplantation Bull, 3*:142-143, 1956.
9. Boyse, E.A., Old, L.J., and Thomas, G.: A report on some observations with a simplified cytotoxic test. *Transplantation Bull, 29*:63-67, 1962.

10. Bennett, B.: Phagocytosis of mouse tumor cells *in vitro* by various homologous and heterologous cells. *J Immun 95*:80-86, 1965.
11. Miller, J.F.A.P.: Role of the thymus in transplantation immunity. *Ann NY Acad Sci, 99*:340-354, 1962.
12. Good, R.A., Dalmasso, A.P., Martinez, C., Archer, O.K., Pierce, J.C., and Papermaster, B.W.: The role of the thymus in development of immunologic capacity in rabbits and mice. *J Exp Med, 116*:773-796, 1962.
13. Waksman, B.H., Arnason, B.G., and Jankovic, B.D.: Role of the thymus in immune reaction in rats. III. Changes in the lymphoid organs of the thymectomized rats. *J Exp Med, 116*:187-206, 1962.
14. Stjernswärd, J.: Immunosuppression by carcinogens. *Antibiot Chemother, 15*:213-233, 1969.
15. Salaman, M.H.: Immunodepression by viruses. *Antibiot Chemother, 15*:393-406, 1969.
16. Malakian, A., and Schwab, J.A.: Immunosuppressant from Group A streptococci. *Science, 159*:880-881, 1968.
17. Malmgren, R.A., Bennison, B.E., and McKinley, T.W.: Reduced antibody titers in mice treated with carcinogenic and cancer chemotherapeutic agents. *Proc Soc Exp Biol Med, 79*:484-488, 1952.
18. Rubin, B.A.: Carcinogen-induced tolerance to homotransplantation. *Progr Exp Tumor Res, 5*:217-292, 1964.
19. Prehn, R.T.: Function of depressed immunologic reactivity during carcinogenesis. *J Nat Cancer Inst, 31*:791-805, 1963.
20. Stutman, O.: Carcinogen-induced immune depression: Absence in mice resistant to chemical oncogenesis. *Science, 166*:620-621, 1969.
21. Brown, G.B., Sugiura, K., and Cresswell, R.M.: Purine N-oxides. XVI. Oncogenic derivatives of xanthine and guanine. *Cancer Res, 25*:986-991, 1965.
22. Teller, M.N., Stohr, G., and Dienst, H.: Studies on the oncogenicity of 3-hydroxyxanthine. *Cancer Res, 30*:179-183, 1970.

Chapter 3

SPONTANEOUS AUTOIMMUNITY IN AGING MICE*

PERRY O. TEAGUE, GEORGE J. FRIOU, EDMOND J. YUNIS,
AND ROBERT A. GOOD

THE results of the studies to be reported here had their beginnings as a search for a serologic and immunopathologic model of systemic lupus erythematosus (SLE), an autoimmune disease which occurs in humans. One of the most characteristic serologic abnormalities in lupus patients is the presence of antinuclear antibodies, termed autoantibodies, since they react with autoantigens (nuclei) *in vitro* resulting in LE cell formation. However, since human antinuclear antibodies also react with purified nuclear materials, we tested for antibodies in mouse serum pools which would react with calf thymus deoxyribonucleoprotein (DNP).

The initial studies were made by surveying sera from seventeen strains of inbred mice obtained from R. B. Jackson Laboratories, Bar Harbor, Maine. All animals were from breeding stocks and were approximately eight months of age. Five pools of sera, ten mice to a pool, were tested in an indirect fluorescent antibody technique. The results of this survey revealed that four of the five pools from strain A/J mice contained anti-DNP antibody. The positive serum pools also contained antibody which reacted with the nuclei of both mouse and human peripheral blood leukocytes in an indirect fluorescent antibody technique.[1]

The tests for anti-DNP antibody were negative in the serum pools of the other strains tested. These strains were A/HeJ, AKR/J, C3H/HeJ, C57L/J, C58/J, DBA/1J, SWR/J, 129/J,

*This investigation was supported in part as various times by U.S.P.H.S. grants A-4750, AM-09703, T1AM-5483, NB-02042, AI-08677, CA-10445, HE-05662, and AI-00292, as well as the American Heart Association and the National Foundation March of Dimes. Part was also done while Dr. Teague was a U.S.P.H.S. Postdoctoral Fellow (F2AI35, 808-01).

C_3HeB/FeJ, $C_{57}BR/cd$, $C_{57}BL/10J$, $C_{57}BL/6J$, RF/J, BALB/cJ, SJL/J, and CBA/J.[1]

Further studies were made on undiluted sera of individual animals of A/J, DBA/1J, and AJDF/1 (F_1 hybrid of A/J females and DBA/1J males) strains. The young A/J and DBA/1J mice were four to six weeks old when purchased. Retired-breeder mice were eight months of age when purchased. The AJDF₁ hybrids were supplied by the supplier of the other mice studied, from the same breeding stock, and maintained there until six months of age. All mice were housed in our laboratory in the same isolated air-conditioned mouse room. The sera of individual male and female mice (50 in each group) of the A/J strain were tested for antibody reactive with DNP and leukocyte nuclei. Similar studies were also carried out on DBA/1J mice. Animals of both strains were eight months of age. Thirty-four percent of the A/J females were found to have anti-DNP antibody. Sera from these mice also reacted with mouse (A/J), rabbit, and human leukocyte nuclei, giving a homogenous pattern of nuclear fluorescence. Sixteen percent of the A/J males were also positive in these tests. None of these A/J sera contained antibody reactive with DNA. None of the serum samples from the fifty male and female DBA/1J mice were found to have anti-DNP or anti-DNA antibodies.[1] Tests with individual sera of $C_{57}BL/6J$ mice revealed that a small percentage of retired breeders had anti-DNP antibody, in contrast to earlier tests with serum pools.[1]

Since one of the characteristic features of the blood of human SLE is LE cell production *in vitro*, a modification of this test was used to determine if A/J mice possessed this autoimmune character. Ten eight-month-old A/J mice which had anti-DNP antibody and ten which were negative were bled. Results of the LE cell tests revealed that six mice were unequivocally positive as indicated by the characteristic pale staining and homogeneity of the ingested material. The A/J mice which lacked anti-DNP were not positive in the LE cell test.[1]

Following these initial observations, it was of interest to determine at what age the capacity for the spontaneous production of autoimmune anti-DNP antibody appeared and if it increased during aging (Table 3-I).[2] In one experiment, fifty A/J males and fifty females (1.5 months of age) were bled at three-week intervals up to 5.5 months of age. None of these mice produced anti-DNP antibody. Thus, it appears from these observations that this spontaneous autoimmune antibody emerges in detectable quantities in A/J mice somewhere between 5.5 and 8 months of age. Sex differences in incidence of anti-DNP antibodies were observed in eight-month-old animals, females greater than males. However, by ten months of age and thereafter, the incidence in all groups of A/J mice increased, and the differences disappeared. By twenty-three months of age, approximately 90 percent of the A/J mice had developed antibody reactive with DNP. Although anti-DNA antibody was not detected in sera of the A/J mice in the 8.5-month, 10-month, or 12-month-old groups, examination of sera from the 23-month-old females revealed that 32 percent of these mice had developed antibody reactive with DNA.

Similar serologic studies were also made with DBA/1J mice. None of the mice examined between 8.5 and 23 months of age developed anti-DNP (Table 3-I) or anti-DNA antibody. Similar negative results were also obtained with sera of various ages of AJDF₁ mice.

The influence of age and strain on antinuclear antibody production was further emphasized in experiments which involved "immunizing" mice with nuclear or other antigens. In one experiment

TABLE 3-I

INCIDENCE OF ANTI-DNP ANTIBODY IN MICE OF VARIOUS AGES
(Adapted from Teague, Friou, and Myers, 1968.[2])

Strain	Group	1.5–5.5	8.5	10	20	23
			Age of Group (months)			
A/J	Female	0*(50)†	13(50)	37(50)	77(40)	
	Female retired breeder		34(50)	44(50)	80(50)	90(50)
	Male	0(50)	10(50)	32(50)	70(50)	
	Male retired breeder		18(50)	40(50)	78(50)	89(50)
DBA/1J	Female		0(53)	0(50)	0(25)	0(25)
	Male		0(53)	0(49)	0(25)	0(25)
AJDF₁	Female		0(40)	0(39)	0(30)	
	Male		0(40)	0(40)	0(33)	

*Percentage of animals with anti-DNP antibody.
†Number of mice in group.

TABLE 3-II

INFLUENCE OF AGE ON ANTINUCLEAR ANTIBODY FORMATION BY FEMALE A/J MICE FOLLOWING TWO WEEKLY IMMUNIZATIONS WITH DNP OR DNA IN FREUND'S COMPLETE ADJUVANT

(Adapted from Teague, Friou, and Myers, 1968.[2])

| | | | | *Sera Reactive with Calf Thymus DNP and/or DNA* | | | | | |
| | | *Before Injection* | | *After One Injection* | | *After Two Injections* | | | |
Age	*Antigen Injected*	*DNP**	*DNA**	*DNP*	*DNA*	*DNP*	*DNA*	*HLN†*	*LE Cells‡*
Months									
4.5	DNP	0/6§	0/6	0/6	0/6	0/6	0/6	0/6	0/6
4.5	DNA	0/6	0/6	0/6	0/6	0/6	0/6	0/6	0/6
4.5	None	0/6	0/6	0/6	0/6	0/6	0/6	0/6	0/6
8	DNP	0/5	0/5	1/5	0/5	4/4‖	0/4	4/4	4/4
8	DNA	0/5	0/5	3/5	0/5	5/5	0/5	5/5	5/5
8	None	0/6	0/6	0/6	0/6	0/6	0/6	0/6	0/6

*Calf thymus DNP or DNA spot test.
†HLN, human leukocyte nuclei.
‡LE cell test.
§Number of positive mice/total number of mice immunized.
‖Number tested decreased because one animal died.

(Table 3-II), 4.5-month-old and 8-month-old female A/J mice were injected with either calf thymus DNP or calf thymus DNA in Freund's complete adjuvant. The presence or absence of both anti-DNP and -DNA antibody activity was determined prior to immunization. Seven days after the first injection, all animals were bled for anti-DNP and -DNA analysis, and then given a second injection. One week later they were bled for similar testing. The results demonstrated that these treatments were unable to induce antinuclear antibody formation in the 4.5-month-old animals. In contrast to the younger mice, immunization evoked in the older mice anti-DNP antibody. None of the immunized animals produced antibody with specificity for DNA even though one group of animals was injected with DNA. All animals that produced anti-DNP antibody after immunization were also positive in the LE cell test. Uninjected control mice for each age group did not develop anti-DNP or -DNA antibodies during the course of the experiment.[2]

Since all materials in this preliminary experiment were combined with complete Freund's adjuvant, a larger experiment was carried out with female and male A/J retired breeders to test the possible influence of the complete adjuvant on the antinuclear antibody responses (Table 3-III). In addition, a group of animals was immunized with heat denatured DNA, and other groups were injected with BSA without adjuvant. None of the animals had detectable anti-DNP antibody prior to injection. All animals were injected on the same day. One week later, they were bled and then all except those that were injected with BSA were given a second injection of the appropriate material. One week later, a serum sample was obtained from all animals. All sera were tested for antibody reactive with calf thymus DNP and/or rabbit thymus DNP spots. With the exceptions of the animals injected with incomplete Freund's adjuvant and the control animals some members of each group produced anti-DNP antibody. All sera which contained antibody reactive with calf thymus DNP also reacted with rabbit thymus DNP, suggesting that this was not a species-specific response. In addition, it is apparent that animals injected only with complete Freund's adjuvant or BSA responded similarly to members in other experimental groups.[2]

TABLE 3-III

SEROLOGIC RESULTS FOLLOWING INJECTION OF EIGHT-
MONTH-OLD A/J MICE LACKING ANTI-DNP ANTIBODY ACTIVITY
(Adapted from Teague, Friou, and Myers, 1968.[2])

| | | Sera Reactive with Calf (CT) and/or Rabbit (RT) Thymus DNP after: | | | |
| | | One Injection | | Two Injections | |
Antigen Injected	Sex	CT DNP	RT DNP	CT DNP	RT DNP
CT DNP	Male	4/6*	4/6	4/6	4/6
CT DNP	Female	3/6	3/6	4/6	4/6
CT DNP in complete Freund's adjuvant	Male	4/6	4/6	4/6	4/6
CT DNP in complete Freund's adjuvant	Female	3/6	3/6	6/6	6/6
CT DNA in complete Freund's adjuvant	Male	5/6	5/6	5/6	5/6
CT DNA in complete Freund's adjuvant	Female	0/5	0/5	3/5	3/5
CT denatured DNA in complete Freund's adjuvant	Male	4/5	4/5	3/5	3/5
CT denatured DNA in complete Freund's adjuvant	Female	2/5	2/5	3/5	3/5
Complete Freund's adjuvant	Male	4/6	4/6	4/6	4/6
Complete Freund's adjuvant	Female	4/6	4/6	4/6	4/6
Incomplete Freund's adjuvant	Male	0/6	0/6	0/6	0/6
Incomplete Freund's adjuvant	Female	0/6	0/6	0/6	0/6
BSA, 40 mg†	Female	2/5	2/5	4/5	4/5
BSA, 2 mg†	Female	2/4	2/4	2/4	2/4
BSA, 20 μg†	Female	2/4	2/4	2/4	2/4
Control, no injection	Male	0/16	0/16	0/16	0/16
Control, no injection	Female	0/16	0/16	0/16	0/16

*Number of positive mice/total number of mice immunized.
†Only one injection of BSA was given; animals were bled when those in all other groups were bled.

An experiment identical to that in Table 3-III was performed with groups of six male and six female DBA/1J retired breeders (8-months-old). The same antigen preparations and experimental protocol were used. It was found that none of these treatments induced DBA/1J mice to produce detectable anti-DNP antibody reactive with either calf or rabbit thymus DNP. In another experiment, a group of six male and six female DBA/1J mice (20-

months-old) and a group of eight male and eight female AJDF₁ hybrids (18-months-old) all lacking antinuclear antibody were given two weekly injections of calf thymus DNP in complete Freund's adjuvant. Sera were obtained one week after the second immunization. None of these sera contained anti-DNP antibodies. It can be concluded from these observations that members of the DBA/1J and the AJDF₁ hybrid strains do not develop the capacity to produce anti-DNP or -DNA antibody either spontaneously or following the immunization procedures used in these experiments.[2]

The observations and experiments described thus far clearly demonstrate that A/J mice express a propensity to produce auto-immune anti-DNP antibody during aging. In contrast, DBA/1J and AJDF₁ never produced anti-DNP or -DNA antibodies either spontaneously or after immunization. It seems important to emphasize that the AJDF₁ hybrids were conceived in A/J females. Therefore, one could assume that the hybrids were exposed to similar internal (*in utero*) as well as external (environmental) factors as the A/J mice studied. Although these studies were not continued throughout the complete life span of all animals, if it is assumed that antinuclear antibody never appeared in the sera of any of the DBA/1J and AJDF₁ hybrid mice during the remainder of their lives, the data could then be interpreted to indicate that the propensity to produce antinuclear antibody, either spontaneously or after antigen injection, is transmitted and/or influenced by genetic factors. A similar suggestion has been advanced to explain the incidence of spontaneous hemolytic disease in both NZB/BL and other strains of mice.[3] Obviously, however, complete understanding of this phenomenon will require extensive genetic analysis.

The immunization experiments, as well as those evaluating the aging animals, demonstrated that the first response in susceptible animals (A/J) is to DNP and not to DNA. In addition, it appears that both strain and age dependent changes must occur if auto-immunity to DNP is to result from the procedures used in this experiment.

Other experiments showed that the responses following the injection of bovine nuclear materials lacked species-specific characteristics since all sera which reacted with calf thymus DNP reacted equally well with rabbit thymus DNP as well as autologous nuclei (LE cells) in some experiments. Anti-DNP antibody was also produced by A/J mice injected with BSA or with complete Freund's adjuvant alone. However, animals injected with incomplete adjuvant as well as uninjected controls did not produce detectable antinuclear antibodies during the experimental period. DBA/1J mice of the same age and given identical treatments were not induced to produce anti-DNP antibody. Older DBA/1J and AJDF1 hybrids were also unresponsive to similar immunizations. Thus, although these experiments do not identify the precise origin or nature of the antigen to which A/J mice responded, they do suggest that the strain and age of the mice were of greater importance than the environmental conditions in influencing the ability to produce anti-DNP antibody. The responses could have been directed against one or more of the following: a) calf thymus DNP, b) nuclear materials of the mycobacteria in the adjuvant, c) trace amounts of protein in the DNA preparation, d) nuclear materials which could have been a contaminant in BSA, e) autochthonous DNP released from damaged tissue either during granuloma formation or by circulating antigen-antibody (i.e. BSA-anti-BSA) complexes, or f) to an unknown microbial agent which was influenced by the experimental procedures. Alternatively, it may be that these treatments simply accelerated genetically influenced processes which had already begun to develop in some mice.

The spontaneous appearance of certain antinuclear antibodies is not unique to A/J mice. Similar serologic reactions have been reported to occur in NZB/BL,[4] F1 hybrid progeny of NZB/BL and certain other strains,[5-7] C57BL/6J,[1] C57BL and C3H,[8] C57BR,[9] and A/HeJ.[10] Antinuclear antibody has also been reported to occur in random bred mice[8] and in dogs.[11] The lag in appearance of antinuclear antibody varies between individual strains of mice. It appears much earlier in NZB/BL mice[8] than in the animals used in our study.

The next phase of these studies was concerned with attempts to transfer adoptively DNP autoimmunity to A/J mice with syngeneic spleen cells. These results revealed that neither the presence nor absence of anti-DNP antibody in the spleen cell donors' sera, nor the viability of the injected cells, was a crucial factor which determined whether or not anti-DNP antibody appeared in the recipient sera. The more-important factor appeared to be the age of the recipient and donor. Data were also collected which implicate that some component of the thymus and spleen (thymus dependent lymphocytes?) is operative in normal animals in "preventing" the spontaneous appearance of autoimmunity.[12]

In all cell transfer experiments, donors and recipients were A/J mice of the same sex. Donor mice were selected on the basis of the presence or absence of anti-DNP antibody. Viable cell suspensions were prepared under sterile conditions from two spleens or four thymuses of each group of donor mice. Suspensions were diluted with medium 199 to contain approximately 4-8 x 10^6 viable mononuclear cells per 0.1 ml. Disrupted cells were prepared by subjecting 0.5-1 ml of viable cell suspension (4-8 x 10^6/0.1 ml of fluid) to three alternate cycles of freezing in a carbon dioxide-ethanol bath and thawing at room temperature. The homogenate was centrifuged at 1000 g for ten minutes and the supernatant used for injection. The sediment and supernatant did not contain intact cells when examined microscopically. Recipient mice were injected intraperitoneally with 0.1 ml volumes of cell preparations or 0.1 ml of medium 199.[12]

In one experiment, groups of seven-week and sixteen-week-old female or male A/J mice were injected with spleen cell preparations derived from retired-breeder mice. The members of each group were injected with either: (a) viable cells from donors with anti-DNP antibody, (b) supernatant from cell homogenate from donors with anti-DNP antibody, (c) viable cells from donors which lacked anti-DNP antibody, (d) supernatant from cell homogenate from donors which lacked anti-DNP antibody, or (e) medium 199. Each animal was bled on a weekly schedule for seven weeks after injection, and each serum sample was tested for anti-DNP antibody. Animals older than sixteen weeks of age were not used as recipients since it had been previously determined that sixteen-week-old A/J mice did not produce anti-DNP antibody after specific immunization.[1, 2] The results of this experiment are contained in Table 3-IV. It was found that adoptive transfer of autoimmunity to DNP can be accomplished in A/J mice, but its success is dependent upon the age of the recipient. A significant

TABLE 3-IV

ANTI-DNP ANTIBODY ACTIVITY IN SEVEN-WEEK-OLD (7-WO) AND SIXTEEN-WEEK-OLD (16-WO) A/J MICE
AFTER INJECTION OF VIABLE SPLEEN CELLS OR SPLEEN HOMOGENATE
DERIVED FROM THIRTY-SIX-WEEK TO FORTY-FOUR-WEEK-OLD
SYNGENEIC DONORS*

(Adapted from Teague and Friou, 1969.[2])

Material Injected†	Donor and Recipient Sex	1		2		3		4		5		6		7	
		7-WO	16-WO	7-WO	16-WO	7-WO	16-WO	7-WO	16-WO	7-WO	16-WO	7-WO	16-WO	7-WO	16-WO
Viable cells, donors anti-DNP+	Female	0/12‡	6/11	0/12	8/11	0/12	7/11	0/12	8/11	0/12	8/11	0/12	8/11	0/12	8/11
	Male	0/11	4/6	0/11	5/6	0/11	3/6	0/11	4/6	0/11	4/6	0/11	4/6	0/11	4/6
Cell homogenate, donors anti-DNP+	Female	0/6	2/5	0/6	3/5	0/6	3/5	0/6	2/5	0/6	2/5	0/6	2/5	0/6	2/5
Viable cells, donors lacked anti DNP	Female	0/12	3/11	0/12	3/11	0/12	4/11	0/12	5/11	0/12	5/11	0/12	6/11	0/12	6/11
	Male	0/11	0/6	0/11	0/5§	0/11	0/5	0/11	0/5	0/11	0/5	0/11	0/5	0/11	0/5
Cell homogenate, donors lacked anti-DNP	Females	0/12	5/11	0/12	4/11	0/12	4/11	0/12	4/11	0/12	4/11	0/12	4/11	0/12	4/11
	Male	0/11	1/6	0/11	1/6	0/11	1/6	0/11	1/6	0/11	1/6	0/11	1/6	0/11	1/6
		0/15	0/13	0/15	0/13	0/15	0/13	0/15	0/13	0/15	0/13	0/15	0/13	0/15	0/13
Medium 199		0/15	0/6	0/15	0/6	0/15	0/6	0/15	0/6	0/15	0/6	0/15	0/6	0/15	0/6

Weeks After Injection

*All recipients lacked anti-DNP antibody before injection.
†The dosage ranged from 6.6×10^6 to 7.8×10^6 viable or homogenized.
‡Number of mice with anti-DNP antibody/total number of mice injected.
§Number of tested mice decreased because one animal died.

number of the older female and male recipients had developed anti-DNP antibody by one week after the cell injection. In contrast, none of the seven-week-old recipients of this or any other experimental group developed anti-DNP after injection. Controls injected with medium 199 did not develop anti-DNP antibody. Two of five recipient females (16-week-old) injected with cell homogenate from donors with anti-DNP antibody developed detectable anti-DNP antibody within one week. These animals remained positive throughout the experiment. Significant numbers of older females injected with viable or disrupted cells from donors which lacked anti-DNP also developed anti-DNP antibody. For example, the number of animals with anti-DNP antibody after the injection of viable spleen cells (donors lacked anti-DNP antibody) increased from three of eleven to six of eleven in six weeks. In contrast, none of the males injected with viable cells, derived from donors which lacked anti-DNP antibody, and only one out of six injected with similar disrupted cells, developed anti-DNP antibody.[12]

In another experiment, groups of eleven thirty-six-week-old female and twelve seventy-two-week-old female retired-breeder A/J mice which had spontaneously developed anti-DNP antibody (+++ antibody activity) were injected with 7.0 x 10^6 viable thymus cells derived from seven-week-old donors. Controls were injected with medium 199. Each animal was bled weekly for six weeks, and each individual serum sample was tested for anti-DNP antibody activity (Table 3-V). Most control animals, initially +++ with respect to anti-DNP antibody, remained +++ during the six weeks of the experiment. A variation of +++ to ++ occurred at least once in four of twelve mice (Nos. 31, 36, 38, and 63). This variation was not considered to be significant. Since results in the controls did not vary on a weekly basis in more than 33 percent of the animals, any variation of ++ or more in the experimental groups was considered to be a significant change. In contrast to the controls, many of the experimental animals apparently had a decrease in the amount of anti-DNP antibody present in their sera. Eight of eleven mice in Group II (Nos. 6, 18, 29, 30, 32, 35, 36, and 46) and six of nine mice in Group III (Nos. 2, 9, 12, 19, 35, and 37) had decreased anti-DNP activity by one to

TABLE 3-V

ANTI-DNP ANTIBODY ACTIVITY IN FEMALE A/J MICE INJECTED
WITH 70 x 10^6 VIABLE THYMUS CELLS DERIVED FROM SEVEN-
WEEK-OLD FEMALE SYNGENEIC DONORS

(Adapted from Teague and Friou, 1969.[12])

Group No.*	Age of Recipient Mouse (Weeks)	Mouse No.	Before Transfer	Anti-DNP Antibody Activity in Recipients Weeks After Transfer					
				1	2	3	4	5	6
I	36	4	+++	+++	+++	+++	+++	+++	+++
		22	+++	+++	+++	+++	+++	+++	+++
		25	+++	+++	+++	+++	+++	+++	+++
		29	+++	+++	+++	+++	+++	+++	+++
		31	+++	+++	++	+++	+++	+++	+++
		36	+++	+++	+++	++	++	+++	+++
		38	+++	+++	+++	++	+++	+++	+++
		49	+++	+++	++	+++	+++	+++	+++
		61	+++	+++	+++	+++	+++	+++	+++
		63	+++	+++	+++	+++	+++	++	+++
		67	+++	+++	+++	+++	+++	+++	+++
		68	+++	+++	+++	+++	+++	+++	+++
II	36	3	+++	+++	+++	+++	+++	+++	+++
		6	+++	−	−	−	−	−	−
		18	+++	−	−	−	−	−	−
		28	+++	++	+	+	++	+++	+++
		29	+++	+	−	−	−	−	−
		30	+++	++	++	+	−	−	−
		32	+++	+	+	−	−	−	−
		35	+++	+	+	+	−	−	−
		36	+++	+	−	−	−	−	−
		38	+++	+++	+++	+++	+++	+++	+++
		46	+++	−	−	−	−	−	−
III	72	2	+++	+	−	−	−	−	−
		7	+++	+	++	D†	D	D	D
		9	+++	+	−	−	−	−	−
		11	+++	+	−	D	D	D	D
		12	+++	+	−	−	−	−	−
		17	+++	+++	++	+	D	D	D
		19	+++	+	−	−	−	−	−
		21	+++	++	++	+	+++	+++	+++
		30	+++	++	++	+	+++	+++	+++
		35	+++	+	−	−	−	−	−
		37	+++	+++	+	+	−	−	−
		38	+++	+++	++	++	+++	+++	+++

*Members of Group I were injected with medium 199; members of Groups II
and III were injected with thymus cells.

†D, animal dead.

three weeks after the injection of thymus cells. Three recipients in Group III died and are not considered. The decrease in anti-DNP antibody in most of the animals was not a transient phenomenon. Animals that became negative remained so throughout the remainder of the experiments.[12]

To test the possible influence of the thymus in "induced" autoimmunity to DNP, groups of nine to ten female and male thirty-six-week-old A/J mice which had not developed anti-DNP antibody spontaneously were injected with viable syngeneic thymus or spleen cells derived from four-week-old donors (Table 3-VI). Controls were injected with medium 199. One, two, and three weeks later all mice were bled and their sera examined for anti-DNP antibody activity. None of these sera contained detectable anti-DNP antibody. None of the animals which had been injected with viable thymus or spleen cells formed antibody to DNP following subsequent immunization with DNP. However, most control mice injected with medium 199 produced anti-DNP following immunization.[12]

TABLE 3-VI

ANTI DNP ANTIBODY ACTIVITY IN THIRTY-SIX-WEEK-OLD A/J MICE AFTER INJECTION OF VIABLE SYNGENEIC THYMUS OR SPLEEN CELLS (4-WEEK-OLD DONORS) AND IMMUNIZATION WITH DNP
(Adapted from Teague and Friou, 1969.[12])

Material Injected	Donor Recipient Sex	Before Transfer	Anti-DNP Antibody Activity in Recipients				
			Weeks After Injection			Weeks After DNP Immunization*	
			1	2	3	1	2
4.7 x 10⁶ thymus cells	Female	0/9†	0/9	0/9	0/9	0/9	0/9
4.4 x 10⁶ thymus cells	Male	0/9	0/9	0/9	0/9	0/9	0/9
7.4 x 10⁶ spleen cells	Female	0/10	0/10	0/10	0/10	0/10	0/10
5.3 x 10⁶ spleen cells	Male	0/9	0/9	0/9	0/9	0/9	0/9
Medium 199	Female	0/10	0/10	0/10	0/10	6/10	9/10
Medium 199	Male	0/10	0/10	0/10	0/10	6/10	7/10

*DNP immunization was given immediately after week 3 sera collections.
†Number of mice with anti-DNP antibody/total number of mice injected.

Thus, aging associated development of autoimmunity to nuclear as well as erythrocyte antigens appears to be a propensity of certain strains of mice but not of others.[13, 4, 1, 5, 3, 8, 2] The mechanism by which spontaneous autoimmunity is induced in experimental animals or humans has not been elucidated; however, several investigations have suggested that the thymus may have an important relationship to the process.[14,15] Its role is revealed by these and other experiments which demonstrate that neonatally thymectomized animals often develop evidence of autoimmunity.[16,17,18,19,20,21,22]

Immunologic evaluation of chickens thymectomized or bursectomized at or prior to hatching, and of mice, rats, and rabbits subjected to neonatal extirpation of thymic or gut epithelium-associated lymphoid tissue has defined two populations of lymphoid cells. One of these is thymus-dependent and subserves the functions of cellular immunity; the other is independent of thymus for its differentiation and subserves the functions of antibody production.[23,24,25,26] Neonatal thymectomy of mice interferes primarily with development or expression of cell-mediated immunities, such as skin allograft and tumor immunity[24,27] and also the capacity to exercise graft-versus-host reactions and to develop delayed allergy.[28] In addition, neonatal thymectomy in mice and rats interferes with production of antibodies to certain antigens even though production of antibodies to many antigens is intact and immunoglobulins are formed normally in neonatally thymectomized animals. Therefore, it seemed appropriate to extend our studies concerned with the thymus, aging, and spontaneous autoimmunity.

We conducted studies on the capacity of mice of various ages to express "thymic-dependent" cellular immunity. We also attempted to determine if there is a relationship of neonatal thymectomy to the propensity for development of autoimmunity during aging. The results revealed that old mice of a strain lacking autoimmune markers retained immunologic vigor throughout life, whereas aging members of strains having propensity to develop autoimmunity showed decreased capacities for certain thymic-dependent immune responses as compared to young animals of the same strain.[29] These observations suggest that the spontaneous appearance of autoimmunity may be associated with a decrease in the functional capacity of the thymus or that of its dependent peripheral lymphoid tissues.

The mice of strains A, C57BL/1, and DBA/2 used in these experiments are produced in a colony, first established by Dr. J. J. Bittner, and subsequently maintained by the late Dr. C. Martinez. NZB mice were obtained from Dr. A. Yamamoto (Cornell Medical Center) at F_{54} and were approximately F_{60} when used. The CBA/H-T6T6 mice were supplied by Dr. K. G. Brand (University of Minnesota).

Animals were surgically thymectomized either within twenty-four hours after birth, at six days of age, or at forty days of age.

Abdominal skin allografts were obtained from forty-five-day to sixty-day-old donors and placed on a prepared site on the back of the recipient by utilizing a standard technique.[30]

Certain mice were injected subcutaneously with 0.2 ml of 20 percent tumor cell suspension from a transplantable sarcoma of strain A or strain C3H origin. The strain A sarcoma (sarcoma 1) was obtained from Jackson Memorial Laboratory, Bar Harbor, Maine, and has been maintained in A/J mice. The C3H sarcoma, kindly provided by Dr. O. Stutman (University of Minnesota) had been isolated from a C3H mouse which had been injected subcutaneously with 7, 12-dimethylbenz(φ)anthracene. The tumor was maintained in syngenic mice and used in passage number 20. All injected test animals were examined daily for the presence of palpable tumors, and growth and regression were recorded.

Both kidneys of strain A mice which had been neonatally thymectomized, thymectomized at six days, or sham-thymectomized were removed at autopsy. One portion of each was fixed in a neutral formalin, and the others were frozen in isopentane precooled in liquid nitrogen. Sections cut from formalin-fixed tissues were stained hematoxylin and eosin and periodic acid-Schiff (PAS). Cryostat sections of the frozen tissues were treated either with fluorescein-labeled anti-mouse δ-globulin or rabbit anti-mouse $\beta_1 C$ globulin, which was prepared by immunizing rabbits with zymosan particles pretreated with fresh mouse serum.[31]

Goat anti-mouse δ-globulin which had been absorbed with appropriate erthrocytes and reticulocytes was used in a direct antiglobulin reaction (Coomb's test) performed on microscope slides. Agglutination was determined by microscopic examination of each specimen.

The *in vitro* responses of mouse spleen cells to PHA were evaluated, with some modification, according to the method described by Lindahl-Kiessling and Peterson.[32]

To determine the incidence of spontaneous antinuclear antibody production in these strains, thirty to forty mice of various ages from strains A and CBA/H-T6T6 and hybrids (NZB x A)F_1 and (A x $C_{57}BL/1$)F_1 were bled. The results of these findings are illustrated in Figure 3-1. None of the CBA/H-T6T6 mice had anti-DNP antibody. In addition, none of these sera contained antibody reactive with DNA, and all tests with washed erythrocytes were negative in the direct Coomb's test (not shown). The (A x $C_{57}BL/1$)F_1 hybrid mice began to develop anti-DNP antibodies between six and eight months of age. The onset was between four and six months in A strain, and between two and three months in the (NZB x A)F_1 hybrids. Although not shown, most animals over one year of age which had anti-DNP antibody also had antibody specifically reactive with DNA.

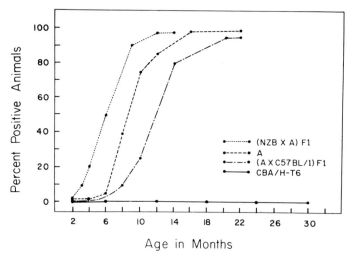

Figure 3-1. Incidence of anti-DNP antibody in aging mice of several strains. (Adapted from Teague *et al.*, 1970.)

In Table 3-VII is contained a summary of studies on the influence of thymectomy on autoimmune hematologic disorders in strains which possess or lack potential for spontaneous autoimmunity during aging. In A strain mice, thymectomy was performed at birth, six days of age, or forty days of age, and sham-

TABLE 3-VII

EFFECT OF THYMECTOMY ON AUTOIMMUNE
HEMATOLOGIC DISORDERS
(Adapted from Teague et al., 1970.[29])

Strain	Treatment	Age days	No. in Group	Lymphocytes* mm³	Hematocrit	Coomb's Test	Antibody Reactive With DNP†	DNA‡
A	Sham neonatal thymectomy	60§	10	3090 ± 595	45.1	0/10	0/10	0/10
		150	10	4625 ± 547	44.6	0/10	0/10	0/10
	Neonatal thymectomy	40-60‖	8	1375 ± 167	37.6	6/8	5/8	5/8
		150¶	8	4779 ± 679	40.5	0/8	4/8	3/8
	Sham 6-day thymectomy	100	19	8481 ± 629	48.2	0/19	0/19	0/19
		160	10	7024 ± 1081	49.0	2/10	1/10	0/10
	6-day thymectomy	100	27	3273 ± 384	46.0	0/27	20/27	7/27
		160	12	2459 ± 261	45.2	8/12	10/12	10/12
	Sham 40-day thymectomy	150	12	5142 ± 786	52.0	0/12	1/12	0/12
	40-day thymectomy	150	12	3974 ± 285	52.3	0/12	9/12	7/12
(AxC57BL)F₁	Sham neonatal thymectomy	135	19	7048 ± 542	48.0	0/19	0/19	0/19
	Neonatal thymectomy	135	19	4549 ± 362	46.5	0/19	11/19	2/19
CBA/H-T6T6	Sham neonatal thymectomy	60	20	9267 ± 1431	49.0	0/20	0/20	0/20
	Neonatal thymectomy	60	12	2473 ± 841	47.3	0/12	4/12	4/12

*Mean ± standard error.
†DNP, deoxyribonucleoprotein.
‡DNA, deoxyribonucleic acid.
§Number positive (total number tested).
‖Wasting animals.
¶Nonwasting animals.

thymectomy controls were also prepared. Neonatal or sham-thy-mectomy was also performed on (A x C57BL/1)F1 hybrid mice and CBA/H-T6T6 mice. In general, lymphopenia was observed in all groups of thymectomized nonwasting 150-day-old mice of strain A. Low hematocrit values were observed in wasting mice of this strain at forty to sixty days of age and in nonwasting 150-day-old thymectomized mice. By contrast, the hematocrits of all other groups were normal. Thymectomy of strain A mice at birth or at six days of age resulted in appearance of Coomb's positive erythrocytes which were not found in most sham-thymectomized controls. Neonatally thymectomized strain A mice which had wasting disease were regularly found to be anemic and most were Coomb's positive. Nonwasting thymectomized, older members of this group were regularly Coomb's negative and were often slightly anemic at five months of age. None of the mice in the remaining (A x C57BL/1)F1 or CBA/H-T6T6 groups were found to have Coomb's positive erythrocytes at the ages tested. Thymectomy of strain A mice at any of the ages tested also led to an accelerated appearance of both anti-DNP and anti-DNA antibodies in comparison to controls. Similar results were also observed in both neonatally thymectomized (A x C57BL/1)F1 hybrids and CBA H-T6T6 animals.

The major histopathologic renal changes observed in strain A mice, which had been thymectomized at birth or six days of age, were alterations in the mesangial cells and perivascular accumulation of lymphoid and plasma cells within the renal parenchyma. These results are tabulated in Table 3-VIII. In the neonatally thymectomized mice, both skin-allografted and nongrafted animals showed renal changes. The glomerular changes varied from a slight enlargement of the mesangium, which appeared to contain excessive amounts of PAS-positive hyaline material, to instances in which the thickened, strongly PAS-positive mesangium appeared to be participating in capillary obliteration, especially in the stalk region. The glomerular capillary basement membranes in advanced lesions also appeared to be thickened. In general, the kidneys showing these changes contained perivascular accumulations of lymphoid cells. Fluorescent antisera to either mouse immunoglobulins or the $\beta_1 C$ component of mouse complement demonstrated the

TABLE 3-VIII

RENAL PATHOLOGY IN THYMECTOMIZED STRAIN A MICE

(Adapted from Teague et al., 1970.[29])

Age	Treatment	Hematoxylin and Eosin	Glomerular Pathology			Perivascular Cellular Infiltrates
			Periodic Acid-Schiff	δ-Globulin*	β1C*	
DAYS						
153	Sham neonatal thymectomy, no skin graft	0/10	0/10	1/8†	1/8†	1/8†
153	Sham neonatal thymectomy, grafted with skin†	0/10	0/10	4/6	0/6	0/10
150	Neonatal thymectomy, no skin graft	1/3	2/3	2/3	1/3	2/3
	Grafted with skin†	2/5	3/5	4/5	3/5	2/5
115	Sham 6-day thymectomy	0/11	0/11	0/11	0/11	1/11
115	6-day thymectomy	2/9	2/9	4/9	2/9	5/9

*Fluorescent microscopy.

†Grafted with (C3H x A)F$_1$ skin at 80 days of age.

presence of abnormal deposits of both these serum proteins. Both mouse immunoglobulins and $\beta_1 C$ appeared to be distributed almost exclusively within the mesangium. A nodular distribution pattern along the basement membranes was not regularly observed. Generally, those experimental animals in which glomerular abnormalities were detected by light microscopy were the ones in which deposits of immunoglobulins and $\beta_1 C$ were found to be present. Control groups of the same ages did not show similar major abnormalities detectable by either light or fluorescent microscopy. However, trace amounts of immunoglobulins were detected within the mesangium of four out of six controls which had recently rejected a skin allograft. As reported previously, aged A/J mice with antinuclear antibodies apparently do develop glomerulonephritis with accompanying deposits of immunoglobulins.[33] For comparative purposes, kidneys of six strain A mice (15 to 17 months of age) were evaluated. Five of these animals had glomerular changes and interstitial accumulation of lymphoid cells appearing identical to those of the thymectomized animals in this study.

TABLE 3-IX

SKIN ALLOGRAFT REJECTION BY MICE OF VARIOUS AGES

Host Strain	Age (Mo.)	Donor Strain	No. in Group	Rejection Time (Days) Mean	± SD*	Range
A	1.5	DBA/2	7	12.8	± 1.73	10-15
	8		5	16.0	± 2.00	14-18
	14		5	19.4	± 3.16	16-23
	17		5	25.2	± 2.45	23-29
NZB	4	DBA/2	6	13.9	± 0.88	13-15
	8		8	14.4	± 3.32	10-20
	10		5	15.6	± 1.73	13-20
	15-17		7	22.7	± 3.16	20-31
(NZB x A)F$_1$	2.5	DBA/2	8	14.4	± 2.65	11-18
	8		6	16.0	± 2.65	11-18
	14		6	20.1	± 5.66	15-30
CBA/H-T6T6	2.5	C3H	14	24.3	± 1.41	21-25
		A	14	21.9	± 2.24	19-26
	8	C3H	14	17.9	± 0.53	16-18
		A	14	17.7	± 1.00	14-18
	22	C3H	15	21.3	± 4.47	19-30
		A	14	23.1	± 1.41	21-26

*SD, standard deviation.

Mice of various ages from strains A, NZB, (NZB x A)F₁, and CBA/H-T6T6 were grafted with allogeneic abdominal skin obtained from young adult donors. As summarized in Table 3-IX, the mean survival time of the allografts on the three "autoimmune" strains (A, NZB, and [NZB x A]F₁) was found to have increased considerably when the older animals of each strain were compared to younger members of the same strain. In contrast, the mean survival times of both strain C₃H and strain A allografts on CBA/H-T6T6 mice of various ages did not show such variation.

Various age groups of mice of strains A, NZB, (NZB x A)F₁, and CBA/H-T6T6 were injected subcutaneously with an allogeneic tumor. As summarized in Table 3-X, the greatest frequency of palpable tumors was observed between five and nine days after tumor cell transplant. In strain A, the fifteen-month and eighteen-month-old groups appeared to have retained the tumors much longer than members of the two younger groups of syngeneic animals. Similar findings were not observed, however, when older and younger NZB, (NZB x A)F₁, and CBA/H-T6T6 mice were evaluated.

The effect of aging on the *in vitro* response of mouse spleen

TABLE 3-X

TUMOR ACCEPTANCE AND REJECTION IN MICE OF VARIOUS AGES*

Strain	Age Mo.	Type of Tumor	No. in Group	Days After Subcutaneous Injection, Number of Mice with Tumor												
				3	5	7	9	11	13	17	20	24	27	30	40	45
A	2.5	C3H	7	2	4	5	5	4	3	0	0	0	0	0	0	0
	9	Sarcoma	5	0	2	3	2	1	1	1	0	0	0	0	0	0
	15		5	0	5	5	4	4	4	4	3	2	2	1	0	0
	18		5	1	4	5	5	5	5	5	4	4	4	3	1	0
NZB	5.5	C3H	6	0	1	0	0	0	0	0	0	0	0	0	0	0
	8–10	Sarcoma	13	1	3	3	0	0	0	0	0	0	0	0	0	0
	16–18		5	0	1	1	0	0	0	0	0	0	0	0	0	0
(NZB	3	C3H	8	2	5	4	0	0	0	0	0	0	0	0	0	0
×	8	Sarcoma	6	2	2	0	0	0	0	0	0	0	0	0	0	0
A)F₁	10		5	2	2	1	0	0	0	0	0	0	0	0	0	0
	14		5	1	1	1	0	0	0	0	0	0	0	0	0	0
CBA/H-	2.5	A	16	3	15	15	15	13	5	4	0	0	0	0	0	0
T6T6	8	Sarcoma I	16	4	12	13	15	16	16	7	6	0	0	0	0	0
	22		14	0	11	11	11	12	14	10	7	1	0	0	0	0

*Adapted from Teague et al., 1970.[29]

cells to PHA stimulation was evaluated in NZB, CBA/H-T6T6, A, and (NZB x A)F_1 mice. In Table 3-XI there is a list of the number of animals tested and the numerical results obtained in separated experiments. Owing to daily variation in the method, numerical comparisons between different strains are not valid. The incorporation of tritiated thymidine into PHA-stimulated cells from old strain A mice did not differ greatly from the younger control animals. The uptake in unstimulated cell cultures, in contrast, was two to three times higher in the animals of this strain. Both the NZB and (NZB x A)F_1 strains showed decreased thymidine uptake in stimulated cultures of the older mice, but no great difference in the unstimulated cultures. In the NZB mice, the reduced response was evident at six months of age. Cell cultures from old CBA/H-T6T6 mice did not differ significantly from those of young syngeneic mice, either stimulated or unstimulated. In general, the variation in response increased with age in all of the strains studied.

Neonatal thymectomy of certain strains of mice has been shown

TABLE 3-XI

EFFECT OF AGE ON THE *IN VITRO* RESPONSE TO
PHYTOHEMAGGLUTININ (PHA) OF MOUSE SPLEEN
CELLS IN DIFFERENT STRAINS*

| | | | Mean c.p.m. | | |
Strain	Age Days	No. of Animals	Control	PHA- Stimulated	p-Value PHA- Stimulated†
A	75	6	3,641	49,027	>0.5
	350	6	3,500	48,942	
	60	2	1,900	42,268	>0.5
	540	6	7,269	41,648	
	90	4	2,929	86,971	>0.5
	630	3	8,523	83,599	
NZB	60	6	2,173	34,331	<0.05
	180	6	1,776	20,917	
(NZB × A)F_1	90	6	3,109	51,222	<0.001
	350	6	2,543	25,649	
CBA/H-T6T6	45	7	2,765	45,457	>0.5
	540	6	2,491	47,007	

*Adapted from Teague *et al.*, 1970.[29]
†Comparison of mean values of old and young mice.

to potentiate the appearance of renal abnormalities[16] which appear identical to those developing spontaneously in aging A/J mice.[32] Studies of patients with systemic lupus erythematosus and accompanying lupus nephritis have revealed a close correlation between active disease and the presence of anti-DNA antibody.[34, 35] Additional studies have established that anti-DNA antibody can be eluted from the immunoglobulin deposits within the glomerulus, and fluorescent antibody studies have revealed that the β1C component of complement and DNA are present within these same deposits.[36] Our findings that strain A mice thymectomized at birth or at six days of age developed anti-DNA antibody and also glomerular lesions containing immunoglobulins and the β1C complement component suggest that this abnormality has resulted from the intravascular formation of anti-DNA-DNA complexes and subsequent renal deposition as seems to be the case in human systemic lupus erythematosus[34, 36] and in (NZB x NZW)F1 hybrid mice.[37] The observation that immunoglobulin deposits were present in trace amounts within the glomeruli of sham-thymectomized strain A mice which had rejected a skin allograft must be considered. This finding may reflect a transient component of the graft rejection process including a humoral response, antigen-antibody-complex formation, and deposition within the mesangial region of the kidneys, which seems to represent a normal pathway for elimination of antigen-antibody complexes.[38, 39]

Prior studies have established that neonatal thymectomy in rodents suppresses development transplantation and tumor immunity,[24, 40-43] formation of antibodies to certain antigens,[24] ability to initiate graft- versus-host reactions,[28, 44] ability to respond to mitogens such as phytohemagglutinin,[45-47] the recovery of lymphoid tissues after irradiation,[48, 49] and the development of normal host-parasite interactions in a conventional environment.[50] In addition, thymectomy in newborn, as well as in adult animals of certain strains, is followed by lymphopenia and fosters development of plasmacytosis in the lymphoid tissues.[22] When certain of these parameters were compared in young and old mice of strain A, deficiencies reminiscent of influences of early thymectomy were often observed. However, considerable variability in the rate of loss of vigor of the thymic immunologic function with age was observed. The strain of mice, the members of which seem to have best retained "thymic-dependent" immune capacities in old age, CBA/H-T6T6, is the strain in which antinuclear antibodies and Coomb's positive erythrocytes do not appear during aging.

Aged animals of strains A, NZB, and (NZB x A)F_1 show a sequential lengthening of the mean rejection time for skin allografts even when a major (H-2) histocompatibility locus is involved. Similar impairment was observed in aging NZB mice for the capacity to initiate graft-versus-host reaction.[51] By contrast, responses of old CBA/H-T6T6 mice to allografts of both H-2 and non-H-2 histocompatibility differences were not different from those observed in younger animals.

Capacity of aged mice to reject tumor allografts was found to be normal in two of the autoimmune strains as well as in the CBA/H-T6T6 mice. However, longer rejection times were found in older strain A mice when compared to younger animals. The number of successful allogeneic tumor takes in animals of each age group of both NZB and (NZB x A)F_1 hybrids was low, a finding which might reflect involvement of strong histocompatibility difference or other nonimmunologic cell interactions[52] that have not been analyzed. At any rate, it was only in the strain A mice that studies of tumor allografts revealed evidence of declining thymus-dependent immunity. On the other hand, the data suggest that older CBA mice reject strain A sarcoma somewhat less well than do younger CBA mice. Further dissection of this apparent discrepancy surely should be conducted.

The mechanism by which PHA induces blast transformation in lymphoid cells is not known; however, much evidence indicates that most lymphoid cells responding to PHA *in vitro* are thymic dependent. Children born with an aplastic or hypoplastic thymus,[53,54] as well as neonatally thymectomized mice[47] and rats,[46] show defective lymphocyte transformation *in vitro*. Conversely, neonatally bursectomized, agammaglobulinemic chickens[55] and also children with hypogammaglobulinemia who have intact cellular immunity[56-58] have normal lymphocyte transformation induced by PHA.

The decrease in PHA-responsiveness occurring with age in the

NZB and (NZB x A)F₁ mice is in keeping with other manifestations of declining cellular immunity observed in these strains.[51] A similar decrease in PHA responsive lymphocytes has been observed with age in humans.[5] In contrast, CBA/H-T6T6 mice, a strain which does not lose cellular immunity with age, also retained their capacity to respond to PHA as late as eighteen months of age. The response observed in old strain A mice is difficult to interpret. The total uptake of tritiated thymidine in stimulated cultures at forty-eight hours was equal to that of the younger animals, but the uptake in unstimulated cultures was at least three times higher in the old animals. Thymidine incorporation in unstimulated culture reflects mainly DNA synthesis which is independent of PHA stimulation. If this is due primarily to the activity of lymphocytes and if the animal is otherwise healthy, then the background is relatively constant after twenty-four hours and can be subtracted from the stimulated cultures or expressed as a ratio of stimulated to unstimulated cultures (s/u). Rate studies performed in old A strain mice[60] indicate that the background activity is not constant and may contain considerable activity related to nonlymphoid cells. Simple ratios or subtraction, therefore, may not be valid under these circumstances, and the significance of the high background activity and the PHA reactivity in cultures from old strain A mice cannot be ascertained at this time.

Previous experiments, similar to these studies concerned with the evaluation of the immune capacity of aging mice have not provided a unified pattern of responsiveness. Aged CBA mice and young syngeneic animals as well rejected strain A skin,[61] but aged CBA mice had decreased numbers of hemolytic plaque-forming cells in their spleen and were less responsive to tumor grafts than were younger animals.[62] The number of C₃H spleen cells with potential to form antibody to sheep erythrocytes was found to decrease markedly during aging.[63] Investigations with aging random bred Swiss mice have demonstrated these animals to have decreased carbon clearance,[64] tumor isoantibody formation,[65] and the capacity to reject skin and tumor allografts.[66] These findings have been correlated with the increase in spontaneous tumor incidence with age.[67] Conflicting results have also been noted when the capacity of aged mice to produce cytotoxic antibody was compared. Aged strain A mice were normal when compared to younger syngeneic animals, whereas aged members of four other strains produced less cytotoxic antibody than did younger syngeneic animals.[67]

It has been postulated that a relationship exists, between the thymus and certain types of autoimmunity.[14,15,68,69] The observation of extensive thymic germinal center formation,[14] and depletion of thymic epithelial cells,[70] in NZB mice have been interpreted to indicate that these histopathologic changes may be directly related to the occurrence of autoimmune disease in members of this strain. However, germinal centers do not develop in the thymus of strain A mice[33] in which autoimmunity to nuclear antigens appears spontaneously[2,12] in incidence equal to that of NZB mice,[8] suggesting that germinal center formation is not of primary pathogenetic significance.

The results obtained with mice subjected to neonatal thymectomy have provoked further conjecture concerning the influence of the thymus in development of autoimmune phenomena. Neonatal thymectomy of NZB mice has usually resulted in an accelerated appearance of Coomb's positive erythrocytes and anemia.[71] Our studies have also shown that by supplying aging A/J mice that had developed anti-DNP antibodies during aging with thymus cells obtained from young syngeneic animals, anti-DNP antibody titers decreased or disappeared completely. Another experiment demonstrated that a component of the spleen (thymus-dependent lymphocytes?) of young A/J mice, when injected into older A/J mice, prevented the induction of autoimmunity to DNP.

The mechanism by which autoimmunity appears either in patients or in certain aging experimental animals has not been resolved by this investigation, although our findings again seem to reflect a relationship among thymus function, immunologic deficiency, and autoimmunity. In this regard, the thymus could act in one of two ways.[1] Vigorous function of the thymic-dependent system could represent a major bulwark against virus and other infective agents and, thus, as a defense against chronic stimulation with antigens which potentially cross-react with host constituents; or alternatively,[2] the thymus may influence, directly or indirectly, a homeostatic system, the function of which is to eliminate abnormal clones of lymphoid cells as they arise by somatic mutation. [14,15] With either mechanism autoimmunity could be associated with immunologic deficiency as may be argued from both clinical and experimental observations.[16,72,17,18,51,19,21,22] The appearance of spontaneous autoimmune phenomena in certain strains of mice, but not in others, may reflect, in part, an instability of either the thymus or a population of lymphoid stem cells responsive to thymus influence, resulting in premature development of one aspect of aging in these animals which is reflected in a disbalance of the immunologic systems similar to that characterizing a thymectomized animal.

REFERENCES

1. Friou, G.J., and Teague, P.O.: *Science, 143*:1333, 1964.
2. Teague, P.O., Friou, G.J., and Myers, L.L.: *J Immun, 101*:791, 1968.
3. Holmes, M.C., and Burnet, F.M.: *Heredity, 19*:419, 1964.
4. Bielschowsky, M., Helyer, B.J., and Howie, J.B.: *Proc Univ Otago Med School, 37*:9, 1959.
5. Helyer, B.J. and Howie, J.B.: *Proc Univ Otago Med School, 39*:17, 1961.
6. Helyer, B.J., and Howie, J.B.: *Brit J Haemat, 9*:119, 1963.
7. Helyer, B.J. and Howie, J.B.: *Nature (London), 197*:197, 1963.
8. Norrins, L.C., and Holmes, M.C.: *J Immun, 93*:148, 1964.
9. Holborow, E.J., Barnes, R.D.S., and Tuffrey, M.: *Nature (London), 207*:601, 1965.
10. Shulman, L.E., Gumpel, J.M., D'Angelo, W.A., Souhami, R.L., Stevens, M.B., Townes, A.S., and Masi, A T.: *Arthritis Rheum, 7*:753, 1964.
11. Lewis, R.M., Schwartz, R., and Henry, W.B.: *Blood, 25*:143, 1965.
12. Teague, P.O., and Friou, G.J.: *Immunology, 17*:665, 1969.
13. Barnes, R.D., and Tuffrey, M.: *Nature (London), 214*:1136, 1967.
14. Burnet, M.: *The Clonal Selection Theory of Acquired Immunity.* Nashville, Vanderbilt University Press, 1958.
15. Burnet, F.M., and Holmes, M.C.: *J Path Bact, 88*:229, 1964.
16. DeVries, M.J., Van Putten, L.M., Balner, H., and Van Bekkum, D.W.: *Rev Franc Etud Clin Biol, 9*:381, 1964.
17. Kellum, M.J., Sutherland, D.E.R., Eckert, E., Peterson, R.D.A., and Good, R.A.: *Int Arch Allerg, 27*:6, 1965.
18. Sutherland, D.E.R., Archer, O.K. Peterson, R.D.A., Eckert, E., and Good, R.A.: *Lancet, 1*:130, 1965.
19. Teague, P.O.: *Fed Proc, 26*:787, 1967.
20. Thivolet, J., Monier, J.C., Ruel, J.P., and Richard, M.H.: *Nature (London), 214*:1134, 1967.
21. Yunis, E.J., Hong, R., Grewe, M.A., Martinez, C., Cornelius, E., and Good, R.A.: *J Exp Med, 125*:947, 1967.

22. Yunis, E.J., Teague, P.O., Stutman, O., and Good, R.A.: *Lab Invest*, 20:46, 1969.
23. Cooper, M.D., Peterson, R.D.A., South, M.A., and Good, R.A.: *J Exp Med*, 123:75, 1966.
24. Good, R.A., Dalmasso, A.P., Martinez, C., Archer, O.K., Pierce, J.C., and Papermaster, B.W.: *J Exp Med*, 116:773, 1962.
25. Jankovic, B.D., and Isakovic, K.: *Int Arch Allerg*, 24:278, 1964.
26. Parrott, D.M.V., De Sousa, M.A.B., and East, J.: *J Exp Med*, 23:191, 1966.
27. Miller, J.F.A.P., Osoba, D., and Dukor, P.: *Ann NY Acad Sci*, 124:95, 1965.
28. Dalmasso, A.P., Martinez, C., and Good, R.A.: *Proc Soc Exp Biol Med*, 110:205, 1962.
29. Teague, P.O., Yunis, E.J., Rodey, G., Fish, A.J., Stutman, O., and Good, R.A.: *Lab Invest*, 22:121, 1970.
30. Martinez, C., Smith, J.M., Aust, J.B., and Good, R.A.: *Proc Soc Exp Biol Med*, 97:736, 1958.
31. Mardiney, M.R., Jr., and Muller-Eberhard, H.J.: *J. Immun*, 94:877, 1965.
32. Lindahl-Kiessling, K., and Peterson, R.D.A.: Presented at the Second Annual Leucocyte Culture Conference, Iowa City, Iowa, 1966.
33. Myers, L., and Friou, G.J.: *Arthritis Rheum*, 8:459, 1965.
34. Casals, S.P., Friou, G.J., and Myers, L.L.: *Arthritis Rheum*, 7:370, 1964.
35. Tan, E.M., Schur, P.H., Carr, R.I., and Kunkel, H.G.: *J. Clin Invest*, 45:1732, 1966.
36. Koffer, D., Schur, P.H., and Kunkel, H.G.: *J Exp Med*, 126:607, 1967.
37. Lambert, P.H., and Dixon, F.J., *J. Exp Med*, 127:507, 1968.
38. Germuth, F.G., Jr., Senterfit, L.B., and Pollack, A.D.: *Johns Hopkins Med J*, 120:225, 1967.
39. Michael, A.F., Fish, A.J., and Good, R.A.: *Lab Invest*, 17:14, 1967.
40. Miller, J.F.A.P.: *Ann NY Acad Sci*, 99:340, 1962.
41. Miller, J.F.A.P.: *The Thymus in Immunobiology*. New York, Harper and Row, 1964
42. Miller, J.F.A.P., Grant, G.A., and Roe, F.J.C.: *Nature (London)*, 199: 920, 1963.
43. Miller, J.F.A.P., Ting, R.C., and Law, L.W.: *Proc Soc Exp Biol Med*, 116:323, 1964.
44. Dalmasso, A.P., Martinez, C., and Good, R.A.: *The Thymus in Immunobiology*. New York, Hoeber Medical Division, Harper and Row, 1964.
45. Dukor, P., and Dietrich, F.M.: *Int Arch Allerg*, 32:521, 1967.
46. Meuwissen, H.J., Van Alten, P.J., and Good, R.A.: *Transplantation*, 7:1, 1969.
47. Rodey, G.E., and Good, R.A.: *Int Arch Allerg*, 36:399, 1969.
48. Globerson, A., and Feldman, M.: *Transplantation*, 2:212, 1964.

49. Miller, J.F.A.P., Doak, S.M.A., and Cross, A.M.: *Proc Soc Exp Biol Med, 112*:785, 1963.
50. Salvin, S.B., Peterson, R.D.A., and Good, R.A.: *J Lab Clin Med, 65*: 1004, 1965.
51. Stutman, O., Yunis, E.J., and Good, R.A.: *Proc Soc Exp Biol Med, 127*:1204, 1968.
52. Hellstrom, K.E.: *Int J Cancer, 1*:349, 1966.
53. Goldman, A.S., Haggard, M.E., McFadden, J., Ritzmann, S.E., Houston, E.W., Bratcher, R.L., Weiss, K.G., Box, E.M., and Szekrenyes, J.W.: *Pediatrics, 39*:348, 1967.
54. Meuwissen, H.J., Bach, F.H., Hong, R., and Good, R.A.: *J Pediat, 72*: 177, 1968.
55. Meuwissen, H.J., Van Alten, P.J., Cooper, M.D., and Good, R.A., *Proceedings of the Third Annual Leucocyte Culture Conference.* New York, Appleton-Century-Crofts, Inc., 1969.
56. Bradley, J., and Oppenheim, J.: *J Clin Exp Immun, 2*:549, 1967.
57. Fudenberg, H.H.: *Hosp. Pract, 3*:43, 1968.
58. Robbins, J.H.: *Experientia, 20*:164, 1964.
59. Pisciotta, A.V., Westring, D.W., DePrev, C., and Walsh, B.: *Nature (London), 215*:193, 1967.
60. Rodey, G.E., and Good, R.A.: Unpublished data.
61. Krohn, P.L.; *Geronotologia, 5*:182, 1961.
62. Stjernsward, J.: *J Nat Cancer Inst, 37*:505, 1966.
63. Makinodan, T.. and Peterson, W.J.: *J Immun, 93*:886, 1964.
64. Aoki, T., Teller, M.N., and Robitaille, M.L.: *J Nat Cancer Inst, 34*:255, 1965.
65. Aoki, T., and Teller, M.N.: *Cancer Res, 26*:1648, 1966.
66. Teller, M.N., Stohr, G., Curlett, W., Kubisek, M.L., and Curtis, D.: *J Nat Cancer Inst, 33*:649, 1964.
67. Teller, M.N., and Eilbert, M.: *Proc Amer Assoc Cancer Res, 7*:71, 1966.
68. Eaton, L.M., and Clagett, O.T.: *Amer J Med, 19*:703, 1955.
69. Mackey, I.R., and de Gail, P.: *Lancet, 2*:667, 1963.
70. DeVries, M.J., and Hijmans, W.A., *J Path Bact, 91*:487, 1966.
71. East, J., and Parrott, D.M.V., *Acta Allerg, (Copenhagen), 20*:227, 1965.
72. Fudenberg, H.H., and Hirschhorn, K.: *Science, 145*:611, 1964.

Chapter 4

THE THYMUS, AUTOIMMUNITY AND THE INVOLUTION OF THE LYMPHOID SYSTEM*

EDMOND J. YUNIS, GABRIEL FERNANDES, PERRY O.
TEAGUE, OSIAS STUTMAN, AND ROBERT A. GOOD

THE appearance of autoantibodies against cellular antigens during aging is a propensity of certain strains of mice but not others.[1-8] In this article we intend to present evidence that the production of these autoantibodies may be related to deficiency of thymic function and/or thymus dependent cells. That the thymus may be related to the pathogenesis of certain autoimmune disorders was suggested by clinical associations of pathologic changes in the thymus and diseases with autoimmune signs, such as myasthenia gravis and systemic lupus erythematosus.[9-11] This hypothesis has also been supported by three separate classes of evidence: (a) Thymic abnormalities are associated with spontaneous autoimmune hemolytic anemia, antinuclear antibodies, and glomerulonephritis in certain mouse strains.[12,13] (b) Reports findings of autoimmune phenomena in thymectomized mice[14-19] and rabbits which had been subjected to extirpation of the central lymphoid tissue during the neonatal period.[20] (c) Similarly thymectomized and irradiated adult rabbits showed a propensity to form autoimmune antibodies.[21] Further, we noted that lymphocyte function was deficient in aging mice of autoimmune susceptible strains. This deficiency was not so prominent in the nonsusceptible strains.[19] These observations also suggested that genetic factors are involved in the involution of the thymus-dependent system and the appearance of autoimmunity. Of further concern

*Supported by grants from the Minnesota and American Heart Associations, the University of Minnesota Graduate School, and the United States Public Health Service (CA-10445 and AI-10153)

is the clinical association of autoimmune phenomena with immune deficiency of man.[11,22]

AUTOIMMUNE SUSCEPTIBLE AND NONSUSCEPTIBLE STRAINS OF MICE

Susceptible strains (NZB, NZW, [NZBxNZW]F_1, A_f^* A/J, and $C_{57}BL/Ks$) and nonsusceptible strains (CBA/H and C_3H_f/Bi) are those strains which develop or do not develop autoantibodies spontaneously during aging. A detail of origin of these strains has been reported elsewhere.[19] Table 4-I shows the increasing frequency of anti-DNP* and anti-DNA antibodies[8] during aging in NZB, NZW, A_f and several hybrid mice prepared between these strains. These mice were weaned at thirty days of age and kept separated throughout the entire experiment. The frequency of anti-DNP antibody in the autoimmune susceptible strains ranged from 17 percent in (NZBxC$_3$H$_f$)F_1 to 82 percent in NZB at twelve months of age. The anti-DNA antibody ranged from 4.3 percent in (NZBx C$_3$H$_f$)F_1 to 59 percent in (NZBxNZW)F_1 at twelve months of age. The autoimmune nonsusceptible strains (CBA/H and C$_3$H$_f$) on the other hand did not show antinuclear antibodies even when examined at eighteen months of age. The incidence of anti-DNP antibody in A_f mice increased from 57 percent at twelve months to 89 percent at eighteen months. Incidence of anti-DNP and anti-DNA was higher in females than in males. The anti-DNP at twelve months in males of all the autoimmune strains was 33 percent, and in females, 58 percent. On the other hand, the incidence of anti-DNA was lower, but showed the same predilection for females in the autoimmune strains, eighteen percent in males and 42 percent in females at twelve months.

Table 4-II summarizes the incidence of antiglobulin reaction of the erythrocytes of several autoimmune susceptible strains. The NZB strain develops rapidly a higher incidence of positive antiglobulin reaction in both sexes than do the other autoimmune strains. At eighteen months the incidence of mice with positive antiglobulin reaction was NZB, 100 percent; (NZBxA$_f$)F_1, 73 percent;

*A_f and C3H$_f$ refer to the strains originated by Bittner free of MTV. A/Umc and C3H/Umc refer to the strains with the MTV. See *Inbred Strains of Mice*, No. 6, page 61, July, 1969.

*Anti-DNP refers to antibodies against nucleoproteins.

TABLE 4-I

DNP AND DNA ANTIBODIES IN DIFFERENT STRAINS OF MICE*

Strain	6 Months						12 Months						18 Months					
	Male		Female		Total %		Male		Female		Total %		Male		Female		Total %	
	DNP	DNA	DNP	DNA	DNP	DNA	DNP	DNA	DNP	DNA	DNP	DNA	DNP	DNA	DNP	DNA	DNP	DNA
(NZB × NZW)F_1	4/7	2/7	7/10	5/10	65	41	5/7	3/7	9/10	7/10	82	59	7/9	0/9	10/10	4/10	89	21
NZB	7/17	2/17	13/15	10/15	62	37	8/14	5/12	9/13	8/11	63	57						
Af	1/11	0/10	3/12	1/10	17	5	6/11	2/11	6/10	2/10	57	19						
NZW	2/12	0/12	3/10	1/10	22	5	3/10	1/9	4/10	4/9	35	28						
(NZB × A)F_1	2/6	0/6	4/10	1/7	37	7	3/10	1/9	5/10	2/6	40	25						
(NZB × C3H)F_1	0/12	0/12	0/12	0/11	0	0	0/12	0/12	4/11	1/11	17	4.3						
C3Hf	0/7	0/7	0/7	0/7	0	0	0/7	0/7	0/7	0/7	0	0	0/4	0/4	1/5	1/5	11	0
CBA/H	0/12	0/12	0/12	0/12	0	0	0/12	0/12	0/10	0/10	0	0	0/8	0/8	0/8	0/7	0	0

*The method described by Teague et al, J Immun, 101:791, 1968.

TABLE 4-II

ANTIGLOBULIN REACTION* OF DIFFERENT STRAINS OF MICE

Strain	3 Months			6 Months			12 Months			18 Months		
	Male	Female	Total %	Male	Female	Total %	Male	Female	Total %	Male	Female	Total %
NZB	14/31	8/25	33.3	25/30	23/30	80.0	20/20	22/25	93.3	6/6	9/9	100
(NZB×Af)F_1	0/31	0/31	0	4/31	3/31	12.9	14/23	8/28	43.1	3/4	5/7	73
(NZB×C3Hf)F_1	0/22	0/20	0	5/22	3/20	19.0	20/28	5/30	43.1	5/10	2/9	37
Af	0/12	0/12	0	1/12	1/12	8	4/11	6/11	45	4/8	6/8	71
C3Hf	0/12	0/12	0	0/12	0/12	0	0/10	0/10	0	0/10	0/10	0
CBA/H	0/12	0/12	0	0/12	0/12	0	0/10	0/10	0	0/10	0/10	0

*Rabbit antimouse serum obtained from Hyland Laboratories, Los Angeles, California. It was absorbed with reticulocyte rich blood following a method described.

$(NZBxC_3H_f)F_1$, 37 percent; and A_f, 71 percent. In the NZB mice the positive antiglobulin reaction is associated with anemia in a large number of animals at six, twelve, and eighteen months of age. The A_f mice showed no anemia at three and six months of age. At twelve months of age the A_f mice with positive antiglobulin reaction showed a mean hematocrit of 39.2, and those with a negative antiglobulin reaction showed a mean hematocrit of 43.8 (Table 4-III). When they were compared individually to the normal controls at two months of age[16, 17] 45.1 ± 2SD 3.24 (See Table 4-IV), there were nine out of ten anemic mice in the group with positive antiglobulin reaction and three out of twelve in the group with negative antiglobulin reaction. It is interesting to observe that mice

TABLE 4-III

HEMATOCRIT LEVELS OF SEVERAL STRAINS OF MICE AT DIFFERENT AGES

		60-90 Days	Antiglobulin	*N° Mice With Anemia*		480-
Strain	N°	Mean ± 2 SD	Reaction	180 Days	360 Days	540 Days
NZB	39*	46.2 ± 5.42	Positive	18/29	12/14	6/6
			Negative	1/6	0/3	— —
A_f	30	45.8 ± 3.51	Positive	0/10	— —	8/12
			Negative	0/18	— —	2/8
$(NZBxA_f)F_1$	27	49.2 ± 4.31	Positive	0/4	0/4	2/4
			Negative	0/12	1/14	4/12
$(NZBxC_3H_f)F_1$	12	47.05 ± 3.86	Positive	0/8	0/10	— —
			Negative	0/14	0/12	— —
CBA-H	10	48.6 ± 4.51	Negative	— —	— —	0/6

*One of seven mice with positive antiglobulin reaction at three months showed anemia.

TABLE 4-IV

RETICULOCYTE COUNTS OF NZB AND A STRAIN OF MICE

	3 Months of Age		Anti-	12-15 Months Mean ± SD	No. of Mice
Strain	Animals in Group	Mean ± SD Reticulocytes %	globulin Test	Reticulocyte %	With High Ret. Count
NZB	12	3.38 ± 1.12	Positive	35.2 ± 10.32	8/8
A_f	12	2.01 ± .82	Positive	5.04 ± 2.17	5/7
			Negative	3.00 ± 1.8	2/8

TABLE 4-V

BONE MARROW AND SPLEEN IMPRINT DIFFERENTIAL COUNTS OF NZB AND A_f MICE OF DIFFERENT AGES

	NZB								A_f								
	Three Months				12-15 Months				Three Months					12-15 Months			
Hematocrit	43.8	46.2	44.3	45.8	25.8	23.0	32.5	45.4	43.8	46.2	48.2	47.3	33	37.8	41.5	45.2	44.0
Reticulocyte %	.7	1.6	2.8	1.2	91	34	27	1.8	2.6	2.3	1.8	2.0	1.3	4.7	7.1	1.8	1.6
Antiglobulin R*	Neg	Neg	Neg	Neg	++++	++++	++++	Neg	Neg	Neg	Neg	Neg	+++	++++	+++	Neg	Neg
Spleen Size**	N	N	N	N	Large	Large	Large	N	N	N	N	N	Large	Large	Large	N	N
Bone Marrow†																	
Blasts	.8	1.4	1.8	1.2	1.2	1.0	2.0	.6	1.2	1.8	1.2	.8	.4	1.2	1.8	1.8	0.8
Myeloid	36.4	40.6	36.2	39.8	24.4	23.6	30.2	40.4	54.6	36.4	55.0	56.8	40.0	52.8	45.2	39.8	51.6
Lymphocytes	27.0	30.0	32.6	29.6	12.2	29.6	19.6	30.6	22.0	34.2	17.2	22.6	43.7	7.2	12.8	30.2	19.2
Histocytes and Mono	.2	.4	.6	1.2	1.0	1.2	1.2	1.2	.8	1.6	.6	2.4	1.2	1.0	.8	2.2	1.0
Plasma Cells	1.0	.6	.8	.8	1.0	.8	.8	Rare	Rare	Rare	Rare	Rare	.4	.2	1.0	.2	1.8
Normoblasts	32.6	24.8	24.2	26.4	59.0	43.0	45.2	27.0	21.0	26.0	24.2	16.6	13.0	36.8	34.0	21.2	23.4
Eosinophils	2.0	2.2	3.8	1.0	1.2	.8	1.0	.2	.4	Rare	1.8	.8	1.4	1.8	2.4	4.6	2.2
Spleen Imprint‡																	
Blasts	.2	Rare	1.6	.8	.6	.8	.6	.4	.8	Rare	1.2	1.0	.2	1.8	1.8	.2	.4
Myeloid	.8	2.8	2.0	2.2	3.0	.4	.2	2.2	5.2	2.2	3.2	1.2	2.8	2.6	8.2	2.0	5.4
Lymphocytes	78.0	79.2	76.6	67.0	55.8	50.6	49.2	90.0	83.2	90.8	82.0	86.0	81.6	76.0	62.2	97.6	86.2
Histocytes and Mono	.4	.8	.6	.2	1.6	.6	.2	2.4	1.8	1.2	1.6	2.8	1.0	.6	1.2	1.2	.2
Plasma Cells	1.4	1.2	1.4	.6	1.8	1.6	.6	Rare	.8	Rare	1.8	0.8	1.2	.8	2.4	.2	.4
Normoblasts	19.2	16.0	17.8	28.2	36.8	46.0	49.2	5.0	8.8	5.8	10.0	8.2	13.2	18.2	24.2	2.0	7.4
Eosinophils	Rare	Rare	Rare	1.0	.4	Rare	Rare	Rare	Rare	Rare	.2	Very Rare	Rare	Rare	Rare	Rare	Rare

*Direct Coombs' Test
**As calculated in Table 8-VI.
†A total of 500 cells was counted. Megakaryocytes can be found.
‡A total of 500 cells was counted. Megakaryocytes and mast cells were found.

with either positive or negative antiglobulin reaction in the (NZBx C₃Hf)F₁ and (NZBxAf)F₁ hybrids did not develop anemia (Table 8-III). The NZB mice with positive antiglobulin test which had anemia at twelve months of age also showed marked reticulocytosis ranging from 18 percent to 91 percent (Table 4-IV). The anemic A_f mice at twelve months of age showed mild reticulocytosis ranging from 1.3 percent to 7.1 percent (Table 4-IV). That the anemia of NZB mice is hemolytic has been shown by several investigations.[2,5] Four of five mice of A_f strain at twelve months of age with anemia and positive antiglobulin reaction showed mild reticulocytosis, and two of eight mice of the negative antiglobulin reaction showed mild reticulocytosis.

Bone Marrow and Spleen Imprints

Bone marrow and spleen imprints were prepared from three months and twelve to fifteen months old NZB and A_f mice following a method described previously.[16]

Table 4-V shows examples of differential counts performed on

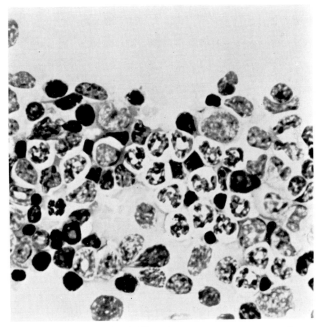

Figure 4-1. Wright-Stained of iliac bone marrow smear from a three-month-old NZB mouse. X400.

smears stained with Wright's stain. There was an increased number of normoblasts in the spleen and bone marrow of three NZB mice with anemia studied at twelve to fifteen months of age (Figs. 4-1-4-4). Two of three of these mice with positive antiglobulin reaction and normal reticulocytes did not show an increase of normoblasts in the bone marrow and spleen. The bone marrow hematoxylin-eosin sections of aging NZB and A_f mice showed good cellularity; the relative increase of normoblasts in the spleen of anemic aging mice of NZB and A_f mice was present in parallel with splenomegaly suggesting that the normoblastosis was not only relative but also absolute. There appeared to be, in addition, an increase of megakaryocytes in spleen and bone marrow in the anemic mice.

The normoblastosis of the spleen and bone marrow in anemic mice is not surprising. The spleen is the main erythropoietic organ in the mouse. The bone marrow is also erythropoietic, but is mainly myelopoietic.[23]

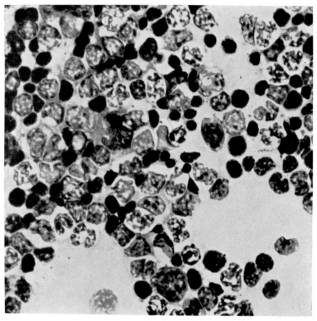

Figure 4-2. Wright-Stain of iliac bone marrow smear from a fifteen-month-old NZB mouse with positive Coombs anemia. Note the large proportion of normoblasts. X400.

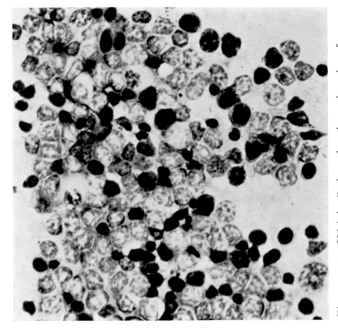

Figure 4-4. Wright-Stain of spleen imprint from a fifteen-month-old NZB mouse with positive Coombs anemia and splenomegaly. Note the large proportion of normoblasts. X400.

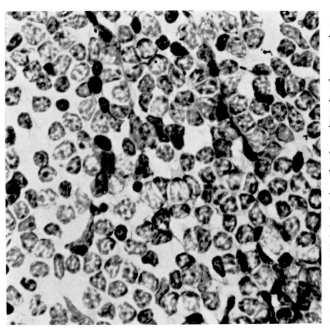

Figure 4-3. Wright-Stain of spleen imprint from a three-month-old NZB mouse. The majority of the cells are lymphocytes. Rare normoblasts and myeloid cells are seen. X400.

Relative Spleen Weights

We have described before the variation of the relative spleen weights in different strains of mice at different ages up to five months of age.[17] The relative spleen weights in NZB, A_f, C_3H_f and CBA/H strains of mice at three months are shown in Table 4-VI. The larger relative spleen weights of females is partly due to the larger body weight of the males. Relative spleen weights higher than the mean $\pm$ 2 standard deviation of the three-month-old groups were considered increased in size.

TABLE 4-VI

RELATIVE WEIGHTS OF SPLEEN AT THREE MONTHS OF AGE

Strain	Female	No. in Group	Male	No. in Group
NZB	513 ± 128	7	477 ± 254	7
A_f	582 ± 166	12	477 ± 186	12
C_3H_f	364 ± 110	12	262 ± 62	12
CBA/H	363 ± 45	12	291 ± 41	12
C57BL/Ks	469 ± 79	12	355 ± 32	12
(C3H × A)F$_1$	373 ± 52	9	323 ± 43	9

Mean ± 2 standard deviations calculated in milligrams per 100 gm of body weight.

TABLE 4-VII

RELATIVE WEIGHTS* OF SPLEEN IN OLD MICE

		12-15 Months Age		20 Months Age	
Strain	Anti-globulin Reaction	Relative Spleen Weight	No Animals Spleno-megaly	Relative Spleen Weight	No Animals Spleno-megaly
A_f	Positive	1,240-1,320-811-716	4/7	816-910-670-1,430	3/4
	Negative	646-415-386			
NZB†	Positive	3,153-3,333-3,214-1,713-1,675-900-837	7/7	1,308-1,509-1,864	3/3
C_3H_f	Negative	405-1,644-385-406-230-420-380	1/7	360-440-428-383-455	0/5
CBA/H	Negative	239-226-336-285-345-400	0/5	310-410-298-322	0/4

*Determined in milligrams per 100 gm of body weight.
†Males.

Gross Postmortem Findings

The spleen weights of eight twelve to fifteen month old NZB mice ranged from 335 mg to 1620 mg, and the spleen weights of three twenty-month-old NZB mice ranged from 820 to 2121 mg. The spleen weights of 4 A$_f$ twenty-month-old mice ranged from 160 to 525 mg. The spleen weights of eight twelve to fifteen-month-old A$_f$ mice ranged from 138 mg to 462 mg. Only one of seven old C$_3$H$_f$ mice showed splenomegaly (due to leukemia). These results are shown in Table 4-VII. All the old NZB mice and eight of eleven old A$_f$ mice showed enlarged lymph nodes. The kidneys of NZB and most A mice appeared pale.

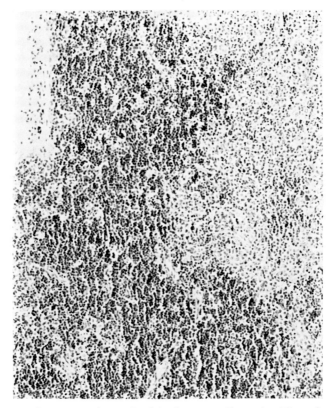

Figure 4-5. Thymus section stained by hematoxylin-eosin. There is enlargement of the medulla with increased number of epithelial cells and histiocytes. Fifteen-month-old NZB. X100.

Microscopic Histopathologic Findings

Thymus

Sections of thymus at twelve to fifteen months of age in NZB mice with anemia showed decreased cellularity of the cortex with widening of the medulla which appeared to have increased number of epithelial cells and histiocytes (Fig. 4-5). Similar findings were seen in the old A$_f$ mice. No "germinal centers" were seen in any of these thymuses.

Lymph Nodes

There was variation in the morphology of lymph nodes between animals and also between lymph nodes obtained from individual

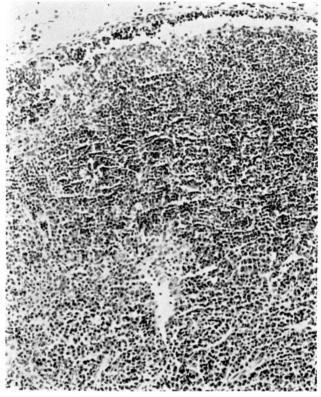

Figure 4-6. Hematoxylin-eosin stained section of mesenteric lymph node from a twenty-month-old A$_f$ mouse. Note the poorly defined lymphatic follicle, the deficiency of lymphocytes in the paracortical portion, and extensive replacement by large number of plasma cells. X100.

mice. There were similarities between the morphology of the lymph nodes of old NZB and most of the strain A$_f$ old mice. Variation in the degree of lymphocyte depletion in the cortex and paracortical areas was present. The germinal centers varied in size; some were enlarged and active. The perifollicular and medullary zones showed a large number of plasma cells and areas of sinus histocytosis (Fig. 4-6, 4-7). One lymph node of an old NZB mouse was replaced by lymphoma (Fig. 4-8). This was the only instance of malignancy observed in this strain.

Spleen

Variation in the size of the lymphatic follicles with widening of the germinal centers was observed with increased number of plasma cells and a decrease of lymphocytes. Most old NZB mice and some old A$_f$ mice showed large numbers of megakaryocytes and normoblasts in the red pulp (Figs. 4-9—4-11). In addition, five of eight old A$_f$ mice (20 months of age) showed perifollicular large histiocytes containing pale eosinophilic material (Fig. 4-12). This material shows positive fluorescence with Thioflavin-T and polarizes after staining with Congo Red. Both NZB and A$_f$ strain of the old group showed phagocytes containing granular coarse brown pigment not unlike hemosiderin about the red pulp.

Liver

A common feature of the liver of old NZB and A$_f$ mice was the findings of periportal inflammatory cells, mainly lymphocytes (Figs. 4-13, 4-14). Two of eight NZB mice of the old group showed foci of degeneration of liver cells with acute inflammatory cells (Fig. 4-14). A few showed enlarged liver cells with large nucleus and a well circumscribed intranuclear inclusion (Fig. 4-15). In six of eight mice of A$_f$ strain we found deposition of amyloid material in Kupffer and endothelial cells and in histiocytes about the central and portal spaces (Fig. 4-16). Foci of lymphocytes were present in these lesions. All NZB and some A$_f$ mice showed Kupffer cells with coarse granular brown material resembling hemosiderin.

Lung

Both strain A$_f$ and NZB mice showed perivascular and peri-

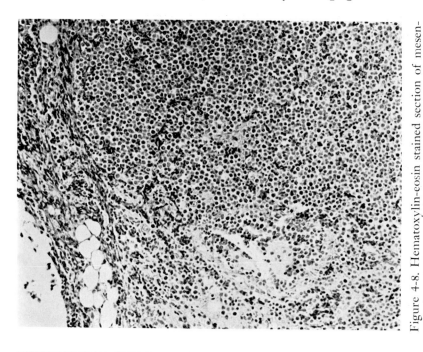

Figure 4-8. Hematoxylin-eosin stained section of mesenteric lymph node from a fifteen-month-old NZB mouse. Note the replacement of the lymph node by cells of uniform size and shape which invade the capsule and pericapsular tissues. X100.

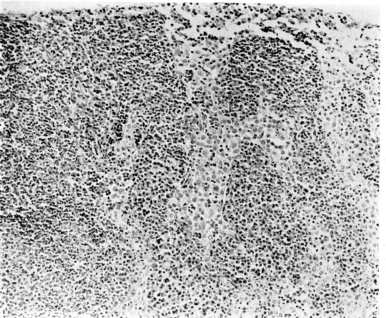

Figure 4-7. Hematoxylin-eosin stained section of mesenteric lymph node from a fifteen-month-old NZB mouse. There is a decrease of lymphocytes and increase of histiocytes and a large number of plasma cells. X100.

Figure 4-10. Spleen section of fifteen-month-old NZB mouse stained by hematoxylin-eosin. The mouse had positive Coombs anemia and splenomegaly. There is a large number of normoblasts. At the lower right corner there is a portion of an enlarged germinal center and deficiency of lymphocytes. X100.

Figure 4-9. Spleen section of fifteen-month-old A_f mouse stained by hematoxylin-eosin. The mouse had positive Coombs anemia and splenomegaly. Note the large number of megakaryocytes and the large number of normoblasts. Note absence of lymphatic follicles. X100.

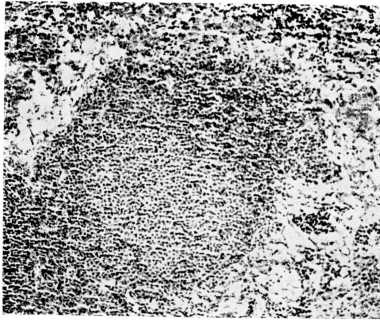

Figure 4-12. Spleen section of twenty-month-old A_f mouse stained by hematoxylin-eosin. Perifollicular amyloidosis of histiocytes. X100.

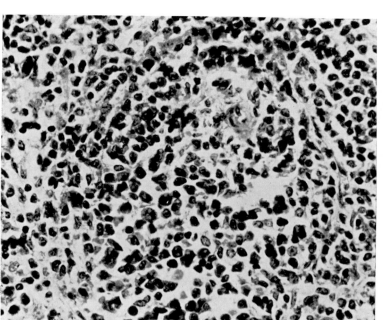

Figure 4-11. Enlarged portion of the same spleen shown in Figure 4-10. Pironin stain showing a small lymphatic follicle replaced by large number of plasma cells. X400.

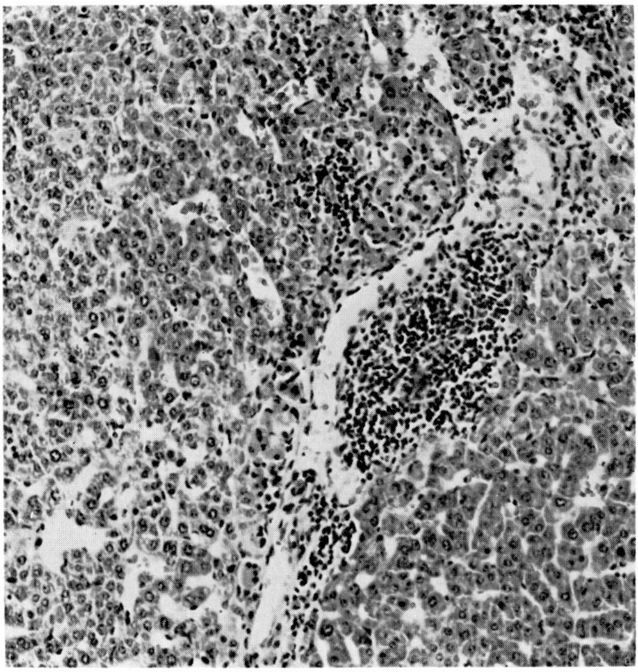

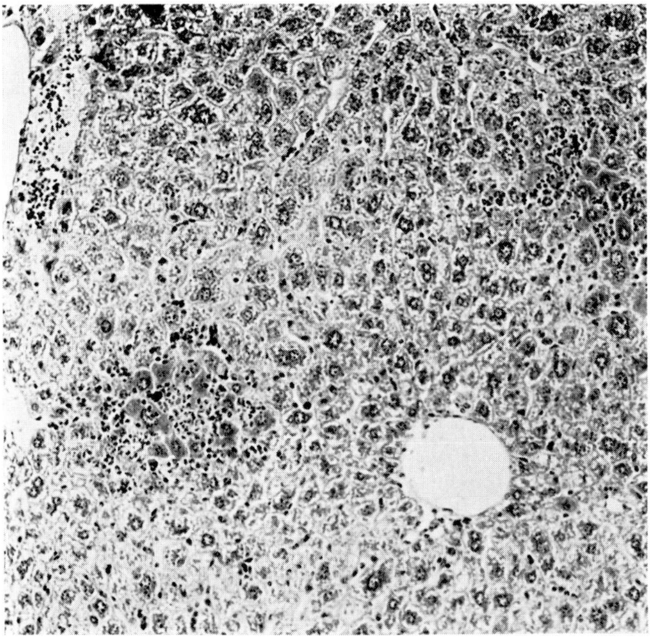

Figure 4-14. Section of liver from a fifteen-month-old NZB mouse showing two foci of inflammation with degenerative changes and periportal infiltration by lymphocytes. Hematoxylin-eosin. X100.

Figure 4-13. Section of liver from a fifteen-month-old A$_f$ mouse showing periportal infiltration of lymphocytes. Hematoxylin-eosin. X100.

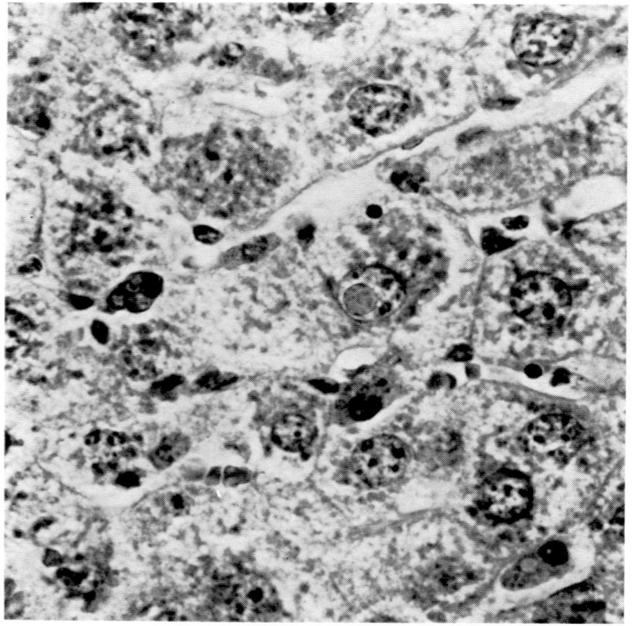

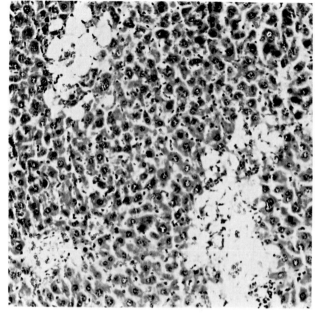

Figure 4-16. Section of liver from a twenty-month-old A$_f$ mouse. Shows intracellular amyloidosis about the central and portal areas. Hematoxylin-eosin.

Figure 4-15. Section of liver from fifteen-month-old NZB mouse. Enlarged portion of the liver from the same mouse of Figure 4-14. There is an intranuclear inclusion body and enlarged Kupffer cells which are filled with brown granular material. X400.

bronchial aggregates of lymphocytes (Fig. 4-17). One of eight strain A$_f$ and one of eight NZB mice had a pulmonary adenoma. In two of the A$_f$ mice and one NZB mouse, pulmonary edema accompanying thickening of the alveolar walls by hyaline eosinophilic material was present.

Intestines

The Peyer's patches of the old A$_f$ and NZB mice show, in some cases, active germinal centers. In some mice depletion of lymphocytes and prominent reticular cells and a few polymorphonuclear leukocytes were found. Deposition of homogenous eosinophilic material giving positive staining for amyloid occurred in the macrophages of the villi of the intestines of the old A$_f$ mice (Fig. 4-18). The amyloid deposits were seen between intestinal glands and also about the blood vessels in small and large intestines of the old A mice.

Kidneys

All eight NZB mice and six of eight A$_f$ mice of the twenty-month-old group showed enlargement of the mesangium containing excessive amounts of PAS positive hyaline material (Figs. 4-19 —4-22). In more severe cases pronounced occlusion of the capillary loops of the glomeruli and areas of scarring of the kidney parenchyma were observed. Foci of perivascular and interstitial accumulations of lymphoid cells were prominent mainly about the corticomedullary junction. Areas of amyloid deposits between the kidney tubules were seen in most of the aging A$_f$ mice (Fig. 4-19).

Other Organs

The pancreas and heart of aging NZB mice did not show remarkable changes. However, in six of eight aging A$_f$ mice, deposition of amyloid occurred between the heart fibers and about the blood vessels.

Immunological Functions of Aging Autoimmune Susceptible Strains

From a functional standpoint, the morphological changes observed with aging in the autoimmune strains are accompanied by deficient immunological functions, especially of the cell-mediated

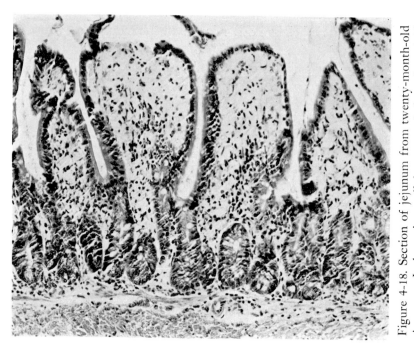

Figure 4-18. Section of jejunum from twenty-month-old A_f mouse. It shows intracellular accumulation of amyloid material in the villi. Hematoxylin-eosin. X100.

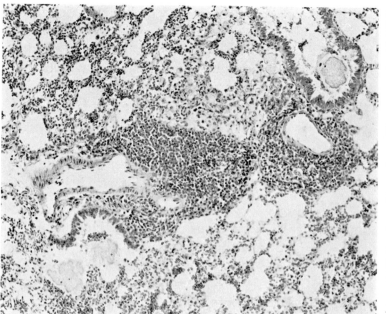

Figure 4-17. Section of lung from fifteen-month-old NZB mouse. Shows perivascular and peribronchial infiltration of lymphocytes and plasma cells. There are areas of pulmonary edema. Hematoxylin-eosin. X100.

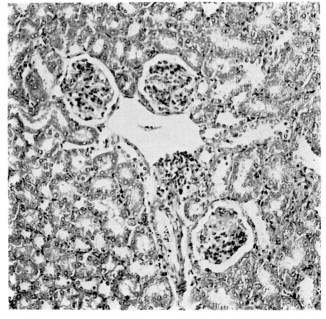

Figure 4-20. Kidney of a twenty-month-old A$_f$ mouse. With hyalynization of the mesangium. Hematoxylin-eosin. Infiltration about corticomedullary vein. X100.

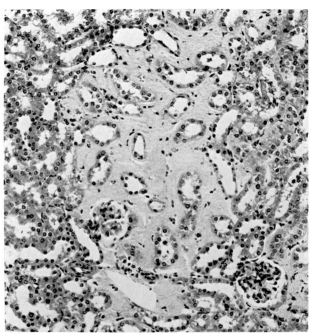

Figure 4-19. Intertubular amyloidosis of kidney obtained from twenty-month-old A$_f$ mouse. Two glomeruli show mesangial homogenous material (not amyloid). Hematoxylin-eosin. X100.

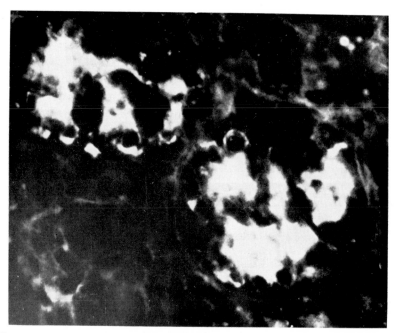

Figure 4-21. Fluorescent microscopic view of two glomeruli of a twenty-month-old A_f mouse. Showing mesangial distribution of host immunoglobulins. X400.

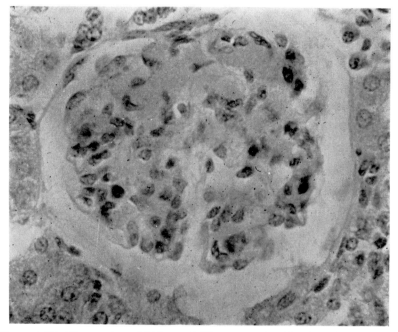

Figure 4-22. Glomerulus of kidney of fifteen-month-old NZB showing PAS positive material in the mesangium. X800.

type, i.e. graft-versus-host reactivity, allograft rejection, and *in vitro* response to phytohemagglutinin or allogeneic cells.[19] Spleen cells from Coombs positive 480-500-day-old male NZB mice were incapable of inducing graft-versus-host reactions when injected into (NZBxA)F_1 hybrids,[24] but younger mice were capable of inducing graft-versus-host reactions in a normal fashion. Increased immunological responses of the humoral antibody type have been described in NZB mice before autoimmunity starts to develop.[25] On the other hand, the immunological defect associated with aging in the nonautoimmune strains (i.e. CBA) is less marked, although detectable.[26]

POSTTHYMECTOMY STATE

Lymphoid Tissues and Lymphocyte Counts

The main finding following neonatal thymectomy of certain experimental animals is depletion of small lymphocytes in the lymphatic tissues, mainly in the paracortical areas of the lymph nodes[27] Figs. 4-23—4-26) and in other thymus dependent regions of spleen

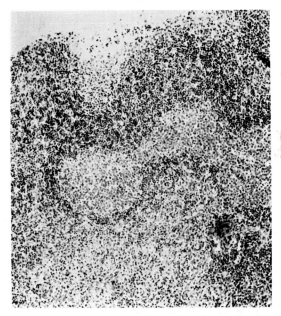

Figure 4-23. Axillary lymph node of a ninety-day-old C3H mouse. Note the lymphatic follicules with germinal center and the large number of paracortical lymphocytes. Hematoxylin-eosin. X40.

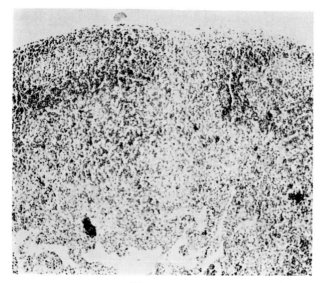

Figure 4-24

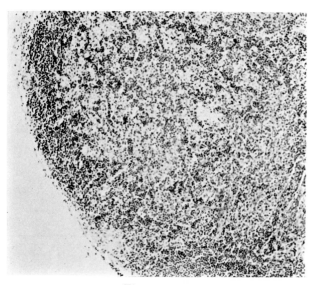

Figure 4-25

and bowel. In addition, lymph nodes and spleen obtained from C₃H neonatally thymectomized mice with wasting disease showed marked cortical atrophy (Figs. 4-26, 4-30).

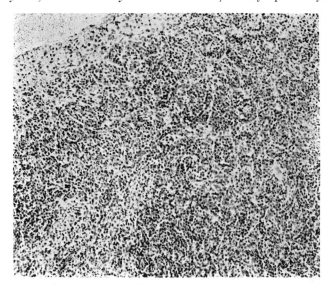

Figure 4-26

Figures 4-24, 4-25, and 4-26. Axillary lymph nodes obtained from three different C3H neonatally thymectomized mice at forty-five to fifty days of age. They show different degrees of lymphocyte depletion of the paracortical areas. Figure 8-26 shows advanced degree of lymphocyte deficiency and lack of follicles. Hematoxylin-eosin. X40.

In contrast, a large number of neonatally thymectomized mice of the autoimmune susceptible strains (NZB, A_f, etc.) showed large lymph nodes and spleen with hyperactive germinal centers, many plasma cells, and increased hemopoiesis (Figs. 4-27, 4-28, and 4-31), and occasionally amyloidosis (Fig. 4-32).

The lymphocyte depletion of lymph nodes, spleen, and Peyer's patches is present in neonatally thymectomized mice of several strains kept in conventional environment and is always more significant in mice with wasting disease than in mice without wasting disease.[17] Neonatally thymectomized mice develop lymphocytopenia which is more pronounced during wasting than in the pre-wasting period (Table 4-VIII). In a relatively small group of mice wasting seemed to be delayed in onset or absent or remained normal up to at least five months, and circulating lymphocyte count returned to almost normal levels at sixty days of age and persisted until five months of age when the animals were sacrificed. None-

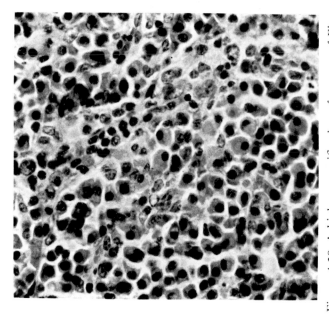

Figure 4-28. A higher magnification of an area of Figure 8-27. Note the large number of plasma cells. Hematoxylin-eosin. X400.

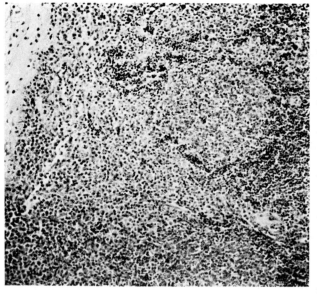

Figure 4-27. Mesenteric lymph node of strain A mouse subjected to neonatal thymectomy and autopsied during wasting at sixty-eight days of age. Note lymphocyte depletion and plasmocytosis. Hematoxylin-eosin. X40.

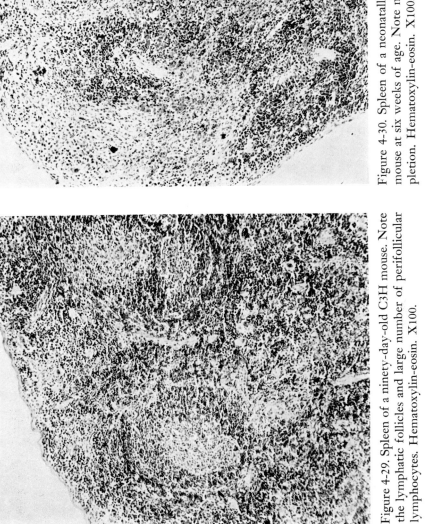

Figure 4-30. Spleen of a neonatally thymectomized C3H mouse at six weeks of age. Note marked lymphocyte depletion. Hematoxylin-eosin. X100.

Figure 4-29. Spleen of a ninety-day-old C3H mouse. Note the lymphatic follicles and large number of perifollicular lymphocytes. Hematoxylin-eosin. X100.

theless, the lymphocyte count may be decreased before mice begin to show evidence of wasting disease.[17]

Cellular Immune System of Neonatally Thymectomized Mice

The neonatally thymectomized mice not only showed quantitative decrease of lymphocytes, but also a qualitative deficiency shown by a deficient ability of suspensions of cells containing lymphocytes to produce graft-versus-host reactions.[28, 29] Further, these animals were deficient in the ability to exercise a normal allograft rejection and to produce delayed hypersensitivity reaction.[30, 31] Neonatally thymectomized A or C3H mice of either

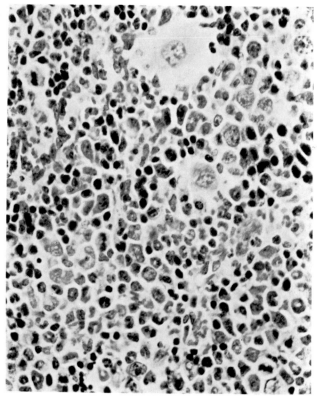

Figure 4-31. Enlarged spleen of a neonatally thymectomized nonwasting strain A mouse sacrificed at 150 days. Note the erythroid and myeloid hyperplasia. Hematoxylin-eosin. X400.

TABLE 4-VIII

LYMPHOCYTE COUNTS IN SHAM AND NEONATALLY THYMECTOMIZED MICE (WASTING AND NOT WASTING)

Lymphocyte Counts*

Age at Test Days		Clinical Condition	No. of Mice	A†	No. of Mice	C3H‡	No. of Mice	NZB	No. of Mice	(NZB $\times$ A_f)F_1
30	Sham Tx	Normal	12	3960 ± 371	21	2453 ± 264				
30	Thymectomy	Not wasting	6	2460 ± 389						
30	Thymectomy	Prewasting	13	1858 ± 234	23	2432 ± 170				
60	Sham Tx	Normal	12	3096 ± 602	12	5570 ± 620	11	2707 ± 482	10	3658 ± 582
35–60	Thymectomy	Wasting	22	1392 ± 166	18	1361 ± 136	8	1677 ± 230	10	1684 ± 411
60	Thymectomy	Normal	15	3521 ± 457						
150	Not operated	Normal	7	3688 ± 413						
150	Thymectomy		9	4373 ± 541						

*Number of cells per cubic millimeter.
†Refers to A/Umc and A_f mice.
‡Refers to C3H/Umc and $C3H_f$ mice.

the wasting or nonwasting variety showed deficiency in ability of their peripheral lymphoid cells to produce splenomegally in F_1 hybrids.[17] Somewhat confusing is the fact that neonatally thymectomized A or C_3H mice with wasting disease which had in addition hepatitis, had by virtue of the infection ability to induce splenomegally in young F_1 hybrids.[17] These false positive tests were not due to influence of the immunocompetent cells, but rather to transmission of infection in the young mice. This view is supported by three sets of observations: In such animals splenomegaly can be induced by supernatant obtained from disrupted cells; splenomegaly can be induced in syngeneic as well as F_1 hybrids; and liver lesions were also observed in the young splenomegalic mice eight days after infection.

Also, neonatally thymectomized A mice did not reject allografts of skin in normal fashion, and both wasting and nonwasting mice showed impaired rejection patterns (Table 4-IX).

TABLE 4-IX

HOMOGRAFT SURVIVAL IN NEONATALLY
THYMECTOMIZED A MICE

	Age	No. Mice	Mean ± SD Survival of Allograft $(C3H \times A)F_1$
Sham Thymectomy	2–3 months	10	13.9 ± .9 days
Neonatal Thymectomy	Wasting (45 days)*	15	36.7 ± 12.2 days
	Nonwasting (150 days)†	5	33.0 ± 11.0 days

*4 mice rejected at 19, 23, 31, and 32 days after grafting. The remaining 11 died without signs of rejection.
†All 5 mice rejected at 20, 20, 35, 45, and 45 days (includes A / Umc and A_f mice).

Wasting Disease in Postthymectomy State

Some neonatally thymectomized mice of several strains developed a wasting syndrome characterized by a failure to gain weight normally or weight loss, hypothermia with hunched posture, diarrhea, and early death (Fig. 4-33). The incidence of postthymectomy wasting varied from strain to strain: 98.5 percent of C_3H, 84.1 percent of A, 71 percent of A_f, 77 percent of (NZBxA)F_1, 71.1 percent of $C_{57}BL/Ks$, 69.2 percent of $C_{57}BL/1$, 65.3 percent of $(C_3HxA)F_1$, 57.8 percent of NZB, 52.6 percent of $(AxC57-BL/1)F_1$, and 52.4 percent of Balb/c mice.

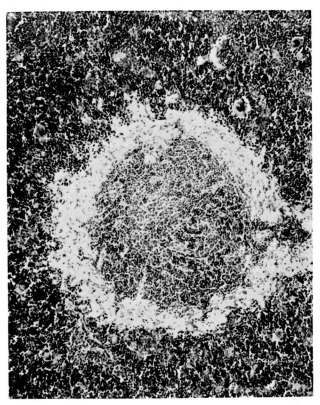

Figure 4-32. Spleen of a neonatally thymectomized nonwasting strain A mouse sacrificed at 150 days. Note the perifollicular amyloid-like material. Hematoxylin-eosin. X100.

Figure 4-33. Strain A_f mice at fifty days of age. Note the hunch appearance and wasting of the one to the left which was thymectomized within twelve hours of birth.

Our mouse colony is filter-barrier pathogen-free, and repeated controls indicated the mice were free of common pathogen bacteria, ectromelia (through repeated vaccinations), and the following viruses: LDH elevating virus, LCM, polyoma, and SV₅.

Occasional Sendai virus titers have been found in our random studies. These controls have been performed with the collaboration of Dr. Bernard A. Briody from the New Jersey College of Medicine.

The role of infections in wasting syndrome of postthymectomy state is strongly suggested by studies of thymectomized mice in germ-free conditions in which no wasting disease was observed,[32, 33] and also, by experiments in which we have shown that 100 percent of the C3H thymectomized mice developed lethal hepatitis when infected with the virus, while normal animals of the same age were resistant to infection.[34] By contrast, hepatitis occurred spontaneously in 32.2 percent of wasting mice of several strains including C3H[17]

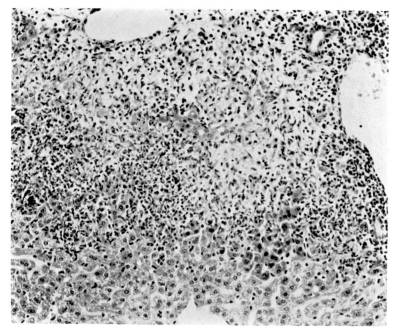

Figure 4-34. Liver of a neonatally thymectomized strain A_f wasting mouse at fifty-three days of age. There is extensive degeneration of parenchymal cells and infiltrates of inflammatory cells. Hematoxylin-eosin. X100.

(Fig. 4-34). Thymectomized mice also show periportal infiltration of lymphocytes and plasma cells (Fig. 4-35). The hepatitis occurring either spontaneously or following injection in neonatally thymectomized mice can be prevented by treatment with thymus grafts, spleen cells, or with grafts of functional thymomas which expand but do not differentiate the lymphoid cells. [34, 35] These experiments suggested that postthymic immunocompetent cells were required to prevent activation of latent virus infections. In addition, we have shown that exhaustion of postthymic cells by injection of Freund's adjuvant in neonatally thymectomized mice increased the incidence and accelerated the appearance of wasting disease and hepatitis in neonatally thymectomized mice.[34] Some neonatally thymectomized mice and rats with wasting syndrome also showed other infections, such as bronchopneumonia.[17, 36]

Thus it seems that variation in expressing the wasting syndrome in neonatally thymectomized mice may be a function of the number of postthymic cells already present in the peripheral lymphoid

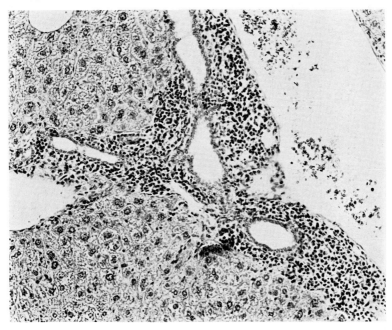

Figure 4-35. Liver of a neonatally thymectomized nonwasting A mouse at 150 days of age. The portal space contains large numbers of plasma cells. Hematoxylin-eosin. X100.

TABLE 4-X

ANTIGLOBULIN REACTION, HEMATOCRITS, AND RETICULOCYTE COUNTS IN NEONATALLY THYMECTOMIZED MICE

Strain	Surgical Treatment	Clinical Condition	Anti-globulin Test*	Age Test Pos	Hematocrit % Mean + SD	No.	No. Anemic Mice	Reticulocyte % Mean + SD	No.
A*	Thymectomy	Wasting	Positive	41–71	35.5 ± 7.14	57	51	2.8 ± 1.63	26
			Negative	41–71	42.4 + 4.27	20	9	2.84 ± 1.17	7
		Not wasting	Positive	60	39.3 ± 2.20	8	7	—	
			Negative	60	41.9 ± 2.91	4	2	—	
			Negative	150	42.0 + 3.60	17	6	—	
	Sham Thymectomy	Normal	Negative	60	45.1 ± 1.62	72	—	3.08 ± .52	32
			Negative	150	44.6 + 1.87	10	—	—	
NZB	Thymectomy	Wasting	Positive	60–90	34.5 ± 4.2	9	8	1.1 ± .95	4
			Negative	60–90	38.9 + 2.52	10	7	.7 ± .5	6
	Sham Thymectomy	Normal	Positive	60–90	46.0 ± 2.64	7	1	1.25 ± .72	5
			Negative	60–90	46.2 ± 2.71	26	—	.9 ± .65	7
C3H	Thymectomy	Wasting	Negative	45	43.93 + 3.52	33	9	2.82 ± 1.3	6
		Not wasting	Negative	45	44.27 + 1.58	10	1	—	
	Sham Thymectomy	Normal	Negative	45	45.6 ± 1.51	19	—	3.25 ± .92	12

*Antimouse serum obtained from Hyland Laboratories, Los Angeles, California.

†Includes A / Umc and A_f mice.

tissue at the time of birth, the amount of exposure to infectious agents, and the amount of stress which has been placed on the poorly developed peripheral lymphoid system which cannot replenish itself.

Autoantibodies in Postthymectomy State

Autoimmune Hemolytic Anemia

We and others[14, 16] have reported previously that thymectomy in susceptible autoimmune strains accelerated the production of Coombs positive anemia. Table 4-X summarizes the results of association between positive antiglobulin reaction and anemia in two autoimmune susceptible strains and in one nonsusceptible. In addition, the means and SD of reticulocyte counts are given in sham operated controls and in the anemic mice to show the lack of reticulocytosis. That the anemia in these mice is hemolytic is confirmed by a decreased ^{51}Cr red cell survival and increase of red cell fragility in hypotonic solutions in some neonatally thymectomized mice with positive antiglobulin reaction.[16] It can also be seen in Table 4-X that there was a low incidence of anemia in wasting and nonwasting neonatally thymectomized mice of susceptible and nonsusceptible strains. These findings suggest that the anemia following neonatal thymectomy may not be solely due to hemolysis asso-

TABLE 4-XI

RELATIONSHIP BETWEEN HEPATITIS AND ANEMIA OF
NEONATALLY THYMECTOMIZED MICE WITH WASTING DISEASE

		Hepatitis and Anemia	*Anemia*	*Hepatitis*	*None*
C3H	Coombs negative	10	3	0	12
A*	Coombs negative	4	3	5	6
	Coombs positive	16	7	1	5
C57BL/Ks	Coombs negative	0	0	0	2
	Coombs positive	6	1	1	5
Total		36	14	8	30

*Includes A/Umc and A_f mice.

TABLE 4-XII

BONE MARROW AND SPLEEN IMPRINTS (NORMOBLASTS %) IN A MICE§

	Sham Thymectomy Age in Days			Neonatal Thymectomy Increase of Normoblasts in Spleen Decrease of Normoblasts in Bone Marrow			
	21	60	150	21 days		41-60 days	150 days
				− Coombs	+ Coombs*	− Coombs†	− Coombs‡
Bone Marrow	26.2-44.0%	20.8-38.4%	22-39.2%	0/8	18/13	5/7	4/7
Spleen Imprints	6.2-28.8%	2.2-12.4%	2.0-15.2%	2/8	9/10	4/5	4/7

*Positive antiglobulin reaction.
†Negative antiglobulin reaction.
‡Negative antiglobulin reaction.
§ = A/Umc and A$_f$ mice.

ciated with the positive antiglobulin test. For instance, there was a high degree of association between liver degenerative and inflammatory lesions and the anemia in A_t, $C_{57}BL/Ks$, and C_3H neonatally thymectomized mice with wasting disease (Table 4-XI). The bone marrow of neonatally thymectomized mice showed a decrease of normoblasts and lymphocytes, not only in mice with positive antiglobulin reaction, but also in mice with negative antiglobulin reaction (Table 4-XII). In addition, normoblastosis of the spleen in neonatally thymectomized mice was regularly observed (Figs. 4-36—4-39). We have suggested that these findings are compatible with the view that neonatally thymectomized mice may produce antibody directed against erythropoietin as suggested in

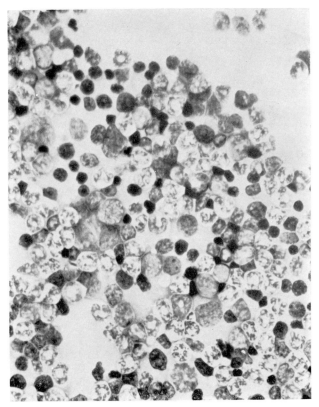

Figure 4-36. Wright-Geimsa stain of normal iliac marrow smear from two-month-old A strain mouse. X500.

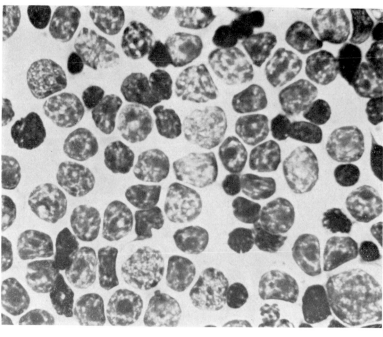

Figure 4-38. Wright-Geimsa stain of spleen imprint from two-month-old A strain mouse. There are few normoblasts and myeloid cells. The majority of the cells are lymphocytes. X100 (oil immersion).

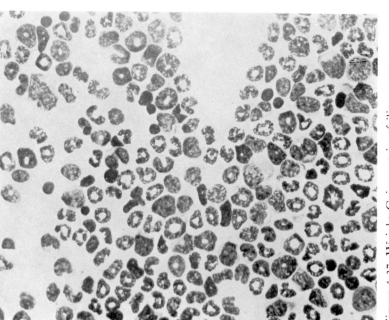

Figure 4-37. Wright-Geimsa stain of iliac marrow smear from fifty-six-day-old neonatally thymectomized A strain mouse with wasting disease, positive Coombs test and anemia. Note the increase of myeloid cells and decrease of normoblasts and lymphoid cells. X500.

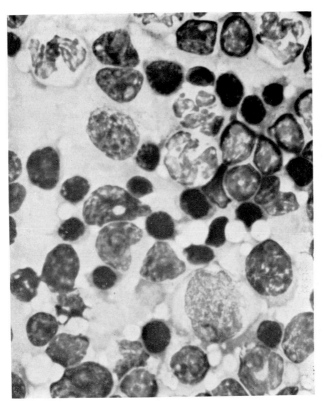

Figure 4-39. Wright-Geimsa stain of spleen imprint from a fifty-two-day-old neonatally thymectomized A strain mouse with wasting disease and splenomegaly. Note the large proportion of erythroid and myeloid cells. X1000 (oil immersion).

patients with thymoma.[37] A second alternative, however, is that hepatitis or other infections in thymectomized animals contribute to the pathogenesis of anemia and normoblastic hypoplasia. This view is suggested by the high correlation between hypoplasia of normoblasts of bone marrow and existence of hepatitis (Table 4-XIII). These findings are interesting since it has been reported that human viral hepatitis is associated with aplastic anemia.[38]

Thus, the peculiar finding of anemia in neonatally thymecto-mized mice, which cannot be explained or is incompletely explained by autoimmune hemolysis and is associated with normoblastic hypo-plasia, finds a reasonable explanation in the susceptibility of neo-

TABLE 4-XIII

RELATIONSHIP BETWEEN HEPATITIS AND NORMOBLASTIC
HYPOPLASIA* OF BONE MARROW OF NEONATALLY
THYMECTOMIZED MICE (A/Umc AND A_f)

		Hepatitis Decreased Normo- blasts	*Decreased Normo- blasts*	*Hepatitis*	*None*
Neonatal Thymectomy (Wasting Disease)	Coombs positive	7	3	1	2
	Coombs negative	3	1	1	1
Neonatal Thymectomy (Nonwasting Disease)	Coombs negative	0	3	0	4

*Normoblastic hypoplasia was determined by a decrease of normoblasts below the lowest normoblasts differential and hypocellularity of the bone marrow.

natal thymectomized mice to agents which may in turn depress development of red blood cells. The paradoxical discrepancy between the neonatally thymectomized mice and the aging mice of the autoimmune strains vis-à-vis normoblastic response in marrow may best be explained on the basis of differences in either exposure to or susceptibility to a virus agent, such as that which can produce both hepatitis and marrow depression.

SPLENOMEGALY. We have previously described that there was splenomegaly in large numbers of mice of the autoimmune suscep-

TABLE 4-XIV

SPLENOMEGALY* IN NEONATALLY THYMECTOMIZED MICE

	Clinical Condition at Sacrifice				
	Wasting	*Nonwasting*			
Strain	*41–71 Days*	*15 Days*	*21 Days*	*60 Days*	*150 Days*
A†	27/40	0/8	9/21	5/9	3/13
C57BL/Ks	4/9			5/8	
(C3H×A)F$_1$	6/10		6/9	1/5	
C3H‡	5/30		3/5		0/3

*Splenomegaly was determined by a relative spleen weight larger than the mean + 2SD as shown in Table VI.
†A/Umc and A_f strains.
‡C3H/Umc and C3H$_f$ strains.

TABLE 4-XV

RELATIONSHIP OF ANEMIA AND SPLENOMEGALY IN NEONATALLY
THYMECTOMIZED STRAIN A* MICE

	Clinical Condition	*No. of Mice With Splenomegaly*
Wasting	Anemia	
35–60	Coombs positive	15/31
Days	Coombs negative	5/10
	Nonanemic	
	Coombs positive	1/6
	Coombs negative	2/8
Nonwasting		
14 Days	Nonanemic	0/8
21 Days	Nonanemic	8/19
150 Days	Anemic	4/6
	Nonanemic	2/7

*A/Umc and A$_f$ mice.

tible strains and the splenomegaly was associated with autoimmune
hemolytic anemia. Table 4-XIV shows that splenomegally was more
frequent in neonatally thymectomized autoimmune strains than
in nonautoimmune strains. Tables 4-XV, and 4-XVI show a high

TABLE 4-XVI

CORRELATION BETWEEN HEPATITIS, ANEMIA AND
SPLENOMEGALY IN WASTING NEONATALLY
THYMECTOMIZED MICE (A/Umc AND A$_f$)

Hepatitis and Anemia	*Anemia*	*Hepatitis*	*No Anemia No Hepatitis*
11/14	19/31	5/8	1/11

correlation between splenomegaly and hepatitis and anemia. Some
nonanemic mice also showed splenomegaly, not only in wasting
disease, but also in nonwasting animals at different ages. At least,
in the wasting group of the neonatally thymectomized mice a correlation exists between splenomegaly and the finding of liver
lesions (Table 4-XVI). Several factors were probably involved in
the production of splenomegaly in these mice: (a) Anemia with
secondary extramedullary hematopoiesis, (b) viral or other infec-

tion leading to extensive plasma cell proliferation, and (c) congestion.

Antinuclear Antibodies

Thymectomy of strain A_f mice at birth or up to forty days of age resulted in an accelerated appearance of anti-DNP and anti-DNA antibodies, and this development was lesser in degree in one nonautoimmune strain studied.[19] Table 4-XVII shows a summary of

TABLE 4-XVII

ANTINUCLEAR ANTIBODIES IN NEONATALLY
THYMECTOMIZED MICE

		Age at Test (Days)	Anti-DNP*	Anti-DNA†
NZB	Neonatal thymectomy	60 w	3/6	–
	Sham thymectomy	60	2/17	–
A‡	Neonatal thymectomy	40–60 w	5/8	5/8
		150	4/8	3/8
	Sham thymectomy	60	0/10	0/10
		150	0/10	0/10
(NZB×A)F$_1$	Neonatal thymectomy	60 w	4/9	–
	Sham thymectomy	60	4/24	–
(A×C57BI$_1$)/F$_1$	Neonatal thymectomy	135 nw	0/19	0/19
	Sham thymectomy	135	11/19	2/19
CBA/H	Neonatal thymectomy	60 w	4/12	4/12
	Sham thymectomy	60	0/20	0/20

*Antibody against deoxyribonucleic acid-protein.
†Antibody against DNA.
‡A/Umc and A_f mice.

the incidence of anti-DNP antibodies in neonatally thymectomized mice of several strains. We have further reported that strain A_f mice thymectomized at birth or at six days of age developed anti-DNA antibody and also glomerular lesions (Figs. 4-40, 4-41) containing immunoglobulins (Fig. 4-42) and B$_1$C (complement component).[19] The nodular type of immunoglobulin and DNA deposition along the epithelial side of the basement membrane which occurs in human systemic lupus erythematosus patients[39, 40] and in (NZBx NZW)F$_1$ mice[41] was not, however, observed in NZB or A_f mice. Instead, the bulk of the immunoglobulin and complement detected was located in the mesangial regions of the glomerular tufts. The basis for differences in distribution of these apparent immunologic com-

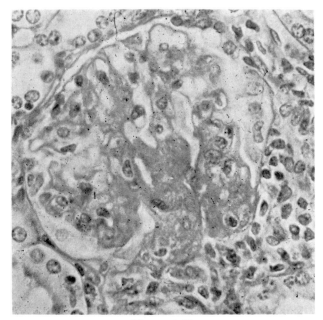

Figure 4-40

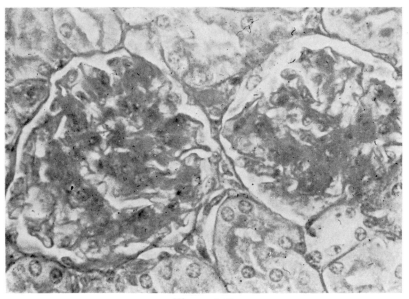

Figure 4-41

Figures 4-40–4-41. Kidney of two neonatally thymectomized nonwasting strain A mice with hyalinization in the tuft and swollen mesangium. Figure 4-41 shows infiltration by round cells. Periodic acid-Schiff. X400.

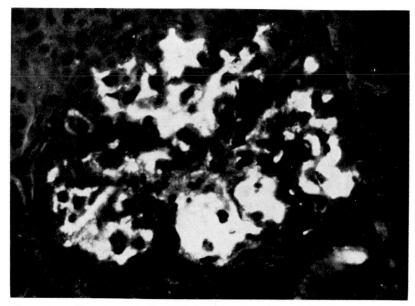

Figure 4-42. Fluorescent microscopic view of a glomerulus of a 150-day-old neonatally thymectomized strain A mouse showing a predominant mesangial distribution of host immunoglobulins. X750.

plexes is not known, but could reflect differences in formation of complexes of variable sizes and physical characteristics in the different experimental animals.[12, 13] These findings are similar to those in aging NZB and A_f mice. In addition, perivascular accumulation within the renal parenchyma of lymphoid and plasma cells was present in five of fifty-two wasting A strain mice and in five of eight nonwasting strain mice at 150 days of age. Other histopathological findings of thymectomized autoimmune susceptible strains which are similar to those described during aging include: histiocytic and plasma cell proliferation of mesenteric lymph node, periportal infiltration of lymphocytes and plasma cells of liver (Fig. 4-37) and peribronchial round cell infiltration of lungs.[17]

In addition, we have described histopathological findings in thymectomized mice of autoimmune susceptible strains that are not found in nonthymectomized mice during aging: crypt lesions of jejunum, ulcerative colitis, degenerative skin lesions, and valvular and myocardial lesions of the heart.[17] In addition, the aging A_f

strain mice showed systemic amyloidosis more regularly than the nonwasting neonatally thymectomized A mice.[17]

These findings suggest that single or multiple infectious processes in immunologically deficient animals could be the primary insult which results in lymphoid depletion and earlier production of auto-immunity in both neonatally thymectomized and aging mice. A relationship between thymus function, cellular immune deficiency and autoimmunity seems apparent. The role of thymectomy in fostering autoantibodies would be primarily based on reduction of normal mechanisms of resistance or surveillance attributable to the thymic dependent system of lymphocytes and cell-mediated immune responses. The thymus-independent plasma cell system could then be excessively stimulated by the antigens derived from infecting agents or exogenous antigens. The autoimmune susceptible strains of mice are prone to develop cellular immune deficiences earlier in life than are the mice not susceptible to autoimmune disease. The nonsusceptible strains also may show autoantibodies following neonatal thymectomy, but they do so in lower frequency than do the autoimmune susceptible strains. These findings suggest the possibility that genetic factors may control the maintenance of the peripheral postthymic lymphoid population and its involution during aging.

REVERSIBILITY OF WASTING DISEASE AND AUTOANTIBODIES OF POSTTHYMECTOMY STATE

We have reported previously that reversal of postthymectomy wasting syndrome in conventional mice can be achieved simply by giving the thymectomized mice a large number of spleen cells or by transplanting to them several thymuses from mature animals.[44-48] Reversal of postthymectomy wasting syndrome is achieved when cells or thymuses are obtained from syngeneic, semi-allogeneic or allogeneic donors sharing the same H_2 histocompatibility locus. When donors of thymuses or cells differ from thymectomized recipients in antigens controlled by the H_2 locus reversal of wasting did not occur, and recipients died of graft-versus-host reaction.[44,47] There are many similarities between the wasting syndromes of the graft-versus-host reaction and that of the postthymectomy state. However, these two conditions differ in that the postthymectomy syndrome can be reversed,[49] but the graft-versus-host reaction cannot be reversed by treatment with syngeneic spleen cells.[49] It has also been argued that graft-versus-host wasting reactions differ from postthymectomy wasting state in that they proceed to lethality in the absence of exogenous microorganisms as in the germ-free environment, whereas neonatally thymecto-mized animals often do not develop wasting in a germ-free environ-ment.[33] Recently however, this view received challenge from the work of Keast,[50, 51] which attributes much of the symptomatology and certainly some of the lethality and pathology to the intestinal flora in the graft-versus-host reaction.

Table 4-XVIII shows a summary of an experiment in which we attempted to compare the reversal of wasting and Coombs positive hemolytic anemia in strain A and $(C_3HxA)F_1$ thymectomized mice. The wasting disease was reversed in 57 percent of A, 66 per-cent of $(C_3HxA)F_1$ and 75 percent of C_3H mice. The mice with Coombs positive test were 78 percent in A and 33 percent in C_3Hx-A. After injection of 200×10^6 spleen cells obtained from syngeneic mice, Coombs tests decreased progressively and became negative by the age of four months.

ATTEMPTS TO REVERSE IN AGING MICE THE DEVELOPMENT OF SPONTANEOUS AUTOANTIBODIES

By supplying A/J mice which developed anti-DNP antibodies during aging with syngeneic thymus cells obtained from young animals, anti-DNP antibody titers decreased or disappeared com-pletely.[52] In another experiment, the spleen of young A/J mice, when injected into older A/J mice, prevented the development of autoimmunity to DNP.[53]

Mice of the A_f strain were treated from the age of one month to the age of eleven months every two months with either 100×10^6 syngeneic spleen cells or one thymus from two-week old syngeneic donors placed intraperitoneally. Controls were injected with 2 ml of Ringer's solution every two months. The antinuclear antibodies (anti-DNP) were studied at six, nine, and fifteen months of age. Treatments with either thymus grafts or syngeneic spleen cells prevented the production of anti-DNP at six months of age. Con-trol mice demonstrated 27 percent positive anti-DNP. At nine

TABLE 4-XVIII

REVERSAL OF POST-THYMECTOMY WASTING AND CONVERSION OF COOMBS
POSITIVE TO COOMBS NEGATIVE BY SPLEEN CELL INJECTION

Strain			Pretreatment 45–60 Days of Age		Posttreatment 45–60 Days		120 Days	
		No.	% Coombs	% Surv.	% Coombs	% Surv.	% Coombs
A_t	Treated	14	78 (11/14)	85 (12/14)	25 (3/12)	57 (8/14)	0
	Control	14	71 (10/14)	36 (5/14)	60 (3/5)	0	0
$(c3H_t \times A_t)F_1$	Treated	6	33 (2/6)	100 (6/6)	17 (1/6)	66 (4/6)	0
	Control	6	50 (3/6)	17 (1/6)	Pos. (1.1)	0	
$C3H_t$	Treated	8	0	75 (6/8)	0	75 (6/8)	0
	Control	7	0	14	0	0	

months and following two treatments, the incidence of anti-DNP was 75 percent in the control group and in the spleen cell treated group, but was 57 percent in the group treated with thymus grafts. There was further increase of incidence of anti-DNP in the control and spleen cell suspension treated groups as opposed to the thymus graft group (Table 4-XIX). At fifteen months of age,

TABLE 4-XIX

ATTEMPTS TO PREVENT ANTINUCLEAR ANTIBODIES IN AGING A$_f$ STRAIN MICE

Treatment*	6 Months Anti-DNP	9 Months Anti-DNP	15 Months Anti-DNP	15 Months Anti-DNA
Ringer's Solution	6/22 (27%)	15/20 (75%)	17/20 (85%)	5/18 (28%)
Spleen Cells†	0/12	19/12 (75%)	9/9 (100%)	7/9 (77%)
Thymus Grafts‡	0/12	4/7 (57%)	3/7 (43%)	3/7 (43%)

**Treatment every 2 months starting at 30 days of age.
†100×10⁶ million spleen cells from strain A$_f$ mice of 2 months of age intraperitoneally.
‡One thymus graft implanted intraperitoneally, obtained from 2-week-old strain A$_f$.

the incidence of anti-DNA antibody was highest in the spleen cell treated group (77%) as opposed to 43 percent of the thymus graft treated group and 28 percent of the control group. Table

TABLE 4-XX

HISTOPATHOLOGIC CHANGES IN A$_f$ MICE* AT 20 MONTHS OF AGE

	Treatment Ringer's Solution	Spleen Cell Suspension	Thymus Grafts
Bronchopneumonia	1/4	1/4	1/5
Amyloidosis of Lung	1/4	1/4	1/5
Amyloidosis of Spleen	1/4	4/6	2/5
Amyloidosis of Liver	3/4	6/6	5/5
Amyloidosis of Intestine	4/4	4/6	3/5
Amyloidosis of Kidney	1/4	2/6	1/5
Amyloidosis of Heart	3/4	6/6	5/5
Myeloid and Normoblastic Hyperplasia of Spleen	2/4	3/6	2/5
Histiocytic and Plasma Cell Proliferation of Lymph Nodes	3/4	4/6	2/5
Mesangial Lesions of Glomeruli	3/4	4/6	2/4

*The mice examined belong to the same experiment described before.

4-XX reviews the histopathologic changes in strain A_f mice which were sacrificed at twenty months of age in this experiment. The result shows that either spleen cell treatments or thymus grafts do not prevent the production of pathological changes which occur in old A_f strain mice.

AGE OF DONOR OF SPLEEN AND RECONSTITUTION OF THYMECTOMIZED MICE

This experiment was designed to test the ability of spleen cells obtained from several ages of autoimmune susceptible and non-susceptible strains of mice to reconstitute syngeneic and allogeneic neonatally thymectomized mice. The experimental model consisted of neonatally thymectozized mice of C_3H_f and A_f strain. At two weeks of age they were treated with 100×10^6 spleen cells obtained from donors of different ages. The strain A neonatally thymectomized mice were treated with spleen cells of strain A donors and the C_3H with spleen cells obtained from CBA/H donors. The CBA/H and C_3H mice share the same H-2 locus 2 (H_2K). Table 4-XXI shows the results of these experiments. The criteria for reconstitution are survivors at six months of age and rejection of skin

TABLE 4-XXI

AGE OF DONOR OF SPLEEN AND RECONSTITUTION OF
THYMECTOMIZED MICE*

Strain	Treatment	6 Month Survivors	Allogeneic Skin Rejection Mean ± SD Days
A_f	100×10^6 2 month A_f	21/22 (95%)	13 ± 1.2 (8)
	100×10^6 12 month A_f	15/19 (79%)	16.7 ± 2.4 (15)
	100×10^6 22 month A_f	0/8	−
	untreated	0/8	−
C3H	100×10^6 2 month-CBA-H	9/9 (100%)	16 ± 2.8 (9)
	100×10^6 23 month CBA-H	5/8 (62%)	13–14–20
	untreated	0/9	−

*Treatment intraperitoneally at 2 weeks of age.

allografts. The A_f mice were grafted with skin from C_3H_f mice, and the C_3H_f mice, skin from A_f mice. The spleen cells obtained from A_f mice of two and twelve months of age produced reconstitution in a larger proportion of mice as compared with spleen cells from twenty-two-month-old A_f mice. In the latter group, for example, all mice died between 80 days and 145 days of age. By contrast, five of eight C_3H_f mice treated with spleen cells obtained from twenty-three-month-old CBA/H donors survived to six months of age, and three mice tested rejected skin allografts at 13, 14, and 20 days as compared to 16 ± 2.8 (SD) days for C_3H_f mice reconstituted with spleen cells from young CBA/H donors. In order to rule out the possibility of infection of the aging mice (22-month-old A_f and 23-month-old CBA/H), 10×10^6 spleen cells of each mouse were injected into newborn mice of the same strain, and these mice survived (23/24 of A_f and 22/24 of C_3H injected with CBA/H).

These results suggest that the spleen cells obtained from old CBA/H donors appear to have greater capacity to restore immunocompetence than do the spleen cells obtained from old A_f mice.

HEMOPOIETIC STEM CELLS IN OLD AND YOUNG BONE MARROW CELLS

In another experiment, bone marrow cells from young (60 to 70-day-old) and aging (460 to 480-day-old) NZB and CBA/H mice were compared for their ability to repopulate lethally irradiated young syngeneic recipients. NZB old mice had positive autoimmune tests. Table 4-XXII shows that the stem cell compartment capable of hemopoietic differentiation is comparable between young and old bone marrow. The number of animals was too small in these experiments to give weight to the apparent higher efficiency of the old bone marrow. The type of hemopoietic colonies formed was also comparable between the two strains and between the two age groups. As reported by others,[54] the majority of the colonies were of erythropoietic type.

THYMIC FUNCTION IN OLD MICE

Thymus grafts from young or old A_f or CBA/H mice were used for reconstitution of neonatally thymectomized mice. Table 4-XXIII shows that aged thymii from A_f or CBA/H were equally

TABLE 4-XXII

POSTIRRADIATION REPOPULATION CAPACITY OF BONE MARROW
CELLS FROM YOUNG AND OLD NZB AND CBA/H MICE

Strain*	Age of BM Donor (Days)	Number of Mice Tested	Relative† Spleen Weight (mg)	Percent Fe59 Uptake in Spleen‡	CFU × 10⁵ Cells§
NZB	no cells	3	162	0.007	0.3
NZB	60–70	3	382	2.7	7.9
NZB	480	5	487	5.9	10.0
CBA/H	no cells	2	158	0.01	0.4
CBA/H	60–70	3	302	3.5	8.8
CBA/H	460	3	286	6.1	10.5

*Seventy-day-old hosts, irradiated with 900R and injected intravenously with 2×10^5 bone marrow cells from syngeneic donors of different ages. Animals sacrificed 8 days after treatment.
†Relative spleen weight corrected for 100 gm of body weight.
‡Injected intraperitoneally with 0.5 mc of Fe59 and sacrificed 6 hours later. Results expressed as percent spleen uptake of total dose.
§Colony forming units counted on histological sections of spleen expressed as CFU per 10^5 injected BM cells.

TABLE 4-XXIII

AGE OF DONOR OF THYMUS AND RECONSTITUTION OF
THYMECTOMIZED MICE*

Strain	Treatment	6-Month Survivors	Allogeneic Skin Rejection (Days)
A_f	2-month A_f	10/22 (45%)	15.1 ± 2.6 (10)
	12-month A_f	7/14 (50%)	16.6 ± 1.9 (8)
	22-month A_f	1/9 (11%)	15 days
C3H	2-month CBA-H	7/10 (70%)	15 ± 2.8 (6)
	23-month CBA-H	1/10 (10%)	> 30

*Treatment intraperitoneally at 2 weeks of age.

ineffective in restoring the thymectomized hosts, indicating comparable degree of functional delay.

On the other hand, we also performed experiments on the duration of thymic function in restored animals. We had observed that in certain strain combinations the thymectomized mice were capable of rejecting the restoring thymus or functional thymoma graft.[55] Table 4-XXIV shows that the restored animals became incompetent with time in absence of thymic function.

TABLE 4-XXIV

DECREASE OF IMMUNOLOGICAL CAPACITIES IN THYMECTOMIZED
C3H MICE GRAFTED WITH STRAIN A THYMOMA THAT
SUBSEQUENTLY REJECTED THE THYMOMA

Experimental Group	No. of Animals	Skin Grafts at 150 Days*		Skin Grafts at 350 Days*	
		A	DBA/2	A 2nd	Balb/c
Normal C3H	10	13.1‡	12.6	12.7	17.3§
		(12–15)	(11–15)	(11–15)	(13–20)
Neonatally Tx. C3H Grafted at 15 Days of Age with A Thymoma†	12	13.5	13.9	37.5	40.4
		(11–17)	(11–16)	(15–50)	(20–50)

*Survival in days, mean and range.
†Rejected the strain A thymoma in 20 to 64 days after grafting.
‡Second set skin grafts from A strain mice at 150 days rejected in 10.3 (9–12) days.
§First set of Balb/c skin at 150 days rejected in 13.3 (12–15) days. A and C3H
include Umc and f strains.

These data indicate that the constant presence of thymic function is essential for the maintenance of the thymus-dependent cell functions.

DISCUSSION

Thymic involution and involution of the thymus-dependent system of cells responsible for cell-mediated immunity occurs in man and all animals which possess a thymus. At the level of the central lymphoid tissue this involution seems to begin at sexual maturity and to continue through adult life into old age. More and more evidence from clinical and laboratory analysis reveals the deficiency of immune functions with age, especially those involving thymus-dependent immune responses. Neonatal thymectomy produces profound defects in cell-mediated immune responses early in life, and the immune deficiencies observed during aging are very similar to those produced or accelerated by neonatal thymectomy.

Thymectomy long after birth in mice and other animals produces an acceleration of development of immune deficit with aging.

In certain strains of mice, NZB for example, profound deficiency of immune function has been shown to develop with aging much earlier in life than with other strains. Among other strains of mice development of immune deficiency with aging is highly variable, and strains of mice can be divided into those in which immune deficiency with age is a more or less prominent feature. Neonatally thymectomized animals as well as aged mice of certain strains show a striking propensity to develop autoimmune phenomena. Indeed, certain strains of mice show the propensity to develop autoimmune phenomena, immunological deficits with aging, and propensity to develop autoimmunity following neonatal thymectomy. Such strains are the NZB and A strains. Rather paradoxically, then, in rabbits, and men and in certain strains of mice immune deficiency and propensity to autoimmunity seem to be associated.

In the development of both immune deficiency and autoimmune phenomena with aging the autoimmune process seems to precede demonstrable development of immune deficiency. However, this is a subtle relationship, and more precise analytical study of immune functions than those used to date may reveal even a closer relationship of these phenomena than have been established at this writing.

On the other hand, it could be, as has been proposed by others, particularly DeVries,[14] that forces contributing to development of autoimmune processes contribute also to development of immune deficiency in neonatally thymectomized animals and during aging. For example, one can cite numerous instances in which viruses capable of establishing chronic infection can influence profoundly immune functions both *in vitro* and *in vivo*. Further, autoantibodies directed against lymphocytes which decrease thymus dependent immune functions have been described.[56,57]

Unifying the observations in this book and our previous publications is the concept that agents present in host or introduced to host from the environment may gain an upper hand in an immune deficient host and contribute to development and expression of autoimmune phenomena. For example, Mellors and others[58-60] have linked an agent present in NZB mice with the autoimmunity as well as the malignancy in this strain. This type of relationship requires further analysis, since in our NZB subline the incidence of lymphomas was extremely low (one in 30 complete autopsies in mice aged from 300 to 480 days). Attempts to produce autoimmune phenomena with "virus" preparations from NZB mice, injected into newborn or young C3H and C57BL/1 mice, gave completely negative results in our hands (Stutman, unpublished). The only positive result observed was the development of lymphoid leukemia at 100-160 days of age in six of sixty-five C3H mice injected as newborns. These data support the evidence that the leukemogenic Gross virus may be the agent involved.[61] The leukemias produced in this way by the NZB "virus" were indistinguishable from the ones produced by Passage A Gross virus. Even more telling have been the experiments of Tonietti, Oldstone, and Dixon[62] which reveal that a variety of chronic virus infections can enhance development of auto-immune phenomena in certain strains of mice, but not in others. Our data would be compatible with the view that the differences in susceptibility of certain strains of mice to development of auto-immunity following neonatal thymectomy or with aging are due to the load of other intrinsic or extrinsic viruses or other agents these strains encounter when they are immunologically defective and to their genetic capability to deal with these infections.

It has been possible in certain experiments to decrease incidence of anti-DNA and anti-DNP antibody in the circulation by giving thymus cells from young animals or to prevent the development of these antibodies with spleen cells from syngeneic animals.[52-53]

Nonetheless, neither thymic transplants from young animals nor repeated injection of spleen cells really influenced development of anti-DNP or histological evidence of autoimmunity in aged mice.

On the other hand, hemopoietic bone marrow stem cells from NZB and CBA/H mice, whether from young or old donors, were equally effective in restoring lethally irradiated syngeneic hosts. We reported previously no differences between the stem cell compartments of normal and thymectomized mice,[63] suggesting a hemopoiesis pathway independent from lymphopoiesis. A report by Trainin et al.[64] indicating deficiency of this stem cell compartment in thymectomized hosts, may be attributed to infection, since we observed that infections, such as mouse hepatitis virus, can depress bone marrow colony forming units, even in normal mice (Stutman, unpublished). It would seem then, that if the stem cell compartment in the aged mouse is spared, the most likely site for the functional involution of the thymus dependent lymphoid tissue may reside in the thymus itself, as is indicated by our preliminary findings (Table 4-XXIII).

These experiments indicate that involution of thymic functions with age may play a role in development of autoimmunity in mice, but also suggest that other factors, such as genetic susceptibility to infections or genetically determined instability of thymus-dependent cell populations, may be involved.

In man, as in animals, autoimmunity goes hand in hand both with genetically determined and acquired immune deficiency and immune deficiency of aging. In man, as in experimental animals, immune deficiencies and certain autoimmune phenomena can be demonstrated as concomitants of aging. Genetically determined immune deficiencies are also accompanied by high frequency of autoimmunity. These include Coombs positive hemolytic anemia, rheumatoid arthritis with or without rheumatoid factors, and diffuse vasculitis.[11, 65, 66] In man, absence of development of the IgA system or deficiencies of this system are accompanied by a high frequency of autoimmunity,[67-72] a finding which suggests that the local antibody system and the IgA system in general may act as a major bulwark against certain food or gut-derived antigenic stimulation, IgA and secretory IgA seem to decrease with aging in man.[73] Whatever its other functions, the IgA system seems to represent a major bulwark against three major classes of viruses.[74-77] In addition, an impaired delayed hypersensitivity in aging population has been found in man.[78] These impairments can be correlated with increasing autoimmunity with aging in man.[79]

The intimate link between immune deficiency and autoimmunity which seems so well explained by the proposal that exogenous agents having antigens that are cross-reactive with those of host could be explained by other hypotheses as well. Burnet and members of his school[80] espouse the view that autoimmune disease is basically a consequence of an immune inadequacy resident in thymus, for example, which permits persistence of clones of cells which otherwise would be eliminated from the body as foreign or abnormal cells. Such clones of immunologically competent cells reacting against host constituents are deemed responsible for the autoantibody and autoimmune diseases. A reverse concept has been proposed by Fudenberg.[22] He feels that clones making autoantibodies are continually arising in normal individuals and are erradicated by their immunological systems. In contrast, such clones are not erradicated in individuals with immune deficiency, either generalized or selective (not detectable by current methods). They proliferate and eventually result in autoimmune disease and/or malignancy. Only extensive further studies will resolve the predictions of these separate hypotheses. Nonetheless, either view is compatible with the observations of an ultimate association of immune deficiency, autoimmunity, and aging emphasized in this paper. It seems likely as a further corollary of these observations that many of the diseases of aging man will be better understood in terms of the immune deficiency and propensity to autoimmunity occurring with aging. An analysis of all pertinent modern data has recently been given by Walford as a background for his own immunologic theory of aging.[81]

SUMMARY

The mechanisms by which autoantibodies or autoimmunity appears either in man or in certain aging experimental animals has not been resolved. However, our findings together with present knowledge seem to reflect a relationship between thymus function, immunologic deficiency, and autoimmunity. Either the thymus or the plasma cell system could act in one of two ways: Vigorous function of the thymic dependent system or the immunoglobulins could represent a major bulwark against virus and other infective agents and, thus, act as immunological surveillance mechanism effective against stimulation with antigens which potentially cross-react with host constituents. Alternatively, the thymus or the plasma cell system may influence directly or indirectly, a homeostatic system, which serves to eliminate abnormal clones of lymphoid cells as they arise by somatic mutation. With either mechanism autoimmunity could be associated with immunologic deficiency as may be argued from both clinical and experimental observations.

The appearance of spontaneous autoimmune phenomena in certain strains of mice, but not in others, may reflect, in part, an instability of either the thymus or thymus-dependent cells, resulting in premature development of one aspect of aging in those animals which is reflected in a disbalance of the immunologic systems similar to that characterizing thymectomized animals. Similarly qualitative deficiencies of immunoglobulins that occur during aging could also produce comparable disbalance.

ACKNOWLEDGMENTS

The authors thank Mr. G. A. Dunn of the Department of Medical Art and Photography of the University of Minnesota Hospitals for his expert assistance in preparing the photomicro graphs.

REFERENCES

1. Barnes, R.D., and Tuffrey, M.: *Nature, 214*:1136, 1967.
2. Bielschowskiy, M., Helyer, B.J., and Howie, J.B.: *Proc Univ Ontago Med School,* 37:9, 1959.
3. Friou, G.J., and Teague, P.O.: *Science, 143*:1333, 1964.
4. Helyer, B.J., and Howie, J.B.: *Proc Univ Ontago Med School, 39*:17, 1961.
5. Helyer, B.J., and Howie, J.B.: *Brit J Haemat, 9*:119, 1963.
6. Holmes, M.C., and Burnet, F.M.: *Heredity, 19*:419, 1964.
7. Norins, L.C., and Holmes, M.C.: *J Immun, 93*:148, 1964.
8. Teague, P.O., Friou, G.J., and Myers, L.L.: *J Immun, 101*:791, 1968.
9. Mackey, I.R., and de Gail, P.: Lancet, 2:667, 1963.
10. Eaton, L.M., and Clagett, O.T.: *Amer J Med, 19*:703, 1955.
11. Wolf, J.K., Gokcen, M., and Good, R.A.: *J Lab Clin Med, 16*:230, 1963.
12. Burnet, F.M., and Holmes, M.C.: *J Path Bact, 88*:229, 1964
13. De Vries, M.J., and Hijmans, W.: *J Path Bact, 91*:487, 1966.
14. De Vries, M.J., Van Putten, L.M., Balner, H., and Van Bekkum, D.W.: *Rev Franc Etudes Clin Biol, 9*:381, 1964.
15. Thivolet, J., Monier, J.C., Ruel, J.P., and Richard, M.H.: *Nature, 214*:1134, 1967.
16. Yunis, E.J., Hong, R., Grewe, M.A., Martinez, C., Cornelius, E., and Good, R.A.: *J Exp Med, 125*:947, 1967.
17. Yunis, E.J., Teague, P.O., Stutman, O., and Good, R.A.: *Lab Invest,* 20:46, 1969.
18. East, J., and Parrott, D.M.V.: *Acta Allerg, 20*:227, 1965.
19. Teague, P.O., Yunis, E.J., Rodney, G., Fish, A.J., Stutman, O., and Good, R.A.: *Lab Invest,* 22:121, 1970.
20. Sutherland, D.E.R., Archer, O.K., Peterson, R.D.A., Eckert, E., and Good, R.A., *Lancet, 1*:130, 1965
21. Kellum, M.J., Sutherland, D.E.R., Eckert, E., Peterson, R.D.A., and Good, R.A.: *Int Arch Allerg,* 27:6, 1965.
22. Fudenberg, H.H.: *Hosp Pract, 3 (no. 1)*:43, 1968.
23. Curry, J.L., and Trentin, J.J.: *Develop Biol, 15*:395-413, 1967.
24. Stutman, O., Yunis, E.J., and Good, R.A.: *Proc Soc Exp Biol Med,* 127:1204, 1968.
25. Morton, J.I., and Siegel, B.V.: *J Reticuloendothel Soc, 6*:78-93, 1969.
26. Krohn, P.L.: *Proc Roy Soc (Biol), 157*:128-147, 1962.
27. Parrott, D.M.V., De Sousa, M.A.B., and East, J.: *J Exp Med, 23*:191, 1966.

28. Dalmasso, A.P., Martinez, C., and Good, R.A.: *Proc Soc Exp Biol Med,* 110:205, 1962.
29. Dalmasso, A.P., Martinez, C., and Good, R.A.: In Good, R.A., and Gabrielson, A.E. (Eds.): *The Thymus in Immunobiology,* New York, Harper and Row, 1964.
30. Miller, J.F.A.P.: *Ann NY Acad Sci, 99:*340, 1962.
31. Stutman, O., Yunis, E.J., and Good, R.A.: *J Nat Cancer Inst, 43:*499, 1969.
32. Wilson, R., Sjodin, K., and Bealmear, M.: *Proc Soc Exp Biol, 117:*237, 1964.
33. McIntire, K.R., Sell, S., and Miller, J.F.A.P.: *Nature (London), 204:*151, 1964.
34. Stutman, O., and Yunis, E.J.: *Am J Path, 59:*81a, 1970.
35. Stutman, O., Yunis, E.J., and Good, R.A.: *Transplantation Proc, 1:*614, 1969.
36. Azar, H.A.: *Proc Soc Exp Biol Med, 116:*817, 1964.
37. Jepson, J.H., and Lowenstein: *Blood, 27:*425, 1966.
38. Rubin, E., Gottlieb, C., and Vogel, P.: *Amer J Med, 45:*88, 1968.
39. Casals, S.P., Friou, G.J., and Myers, L.L.: *Arthritis Rheum, 7:*379, 1964.
40. Koffler, D., Schur, P.H., and Kunkel, H.G.: *J Exp Med, 126:*607, 1967.
41. Lambert, P.H., and Dixon, F.J.: *J Exp Med, 127:*507, 1968.
42. Germuth, F.G., Jr., Senterfit, L.B., and Pollack, A.D.: *Johns Hopkins Med J., 120:*225, 1967.
43. Michael, A.F., Fish, A.J., and Good, R.A.: *Lab Invest, 17:*14, 1967.
44. Yunis, E.J., Hilgard, H.R., Martinez, C., and Good, R.A.: *J Exp Med, 121:*607, 1965.
45. Stutman, O., Yunis, E.J., Martinez, C., and Good, R.A.: *J Immun, 98:*79-87, 1967.
46. Stutman, O., Yunis, E.J., and Good, R.A.: *J Immun, 102:*87-92, 1969.
47. Stutman, O., Yunis, E.J., and Good, R.A.: *Transplantation, 7:*420, 1969.
48. Stutman, O., Yunis, E.J., and Good, R.A.: *J Exp Med, 130:*809-819, 1969.
49. Stutman, O., Yunis, E.J., Teague, P.O., and Good, R.A.: *Transplantation, 6:*514-523, 1968.
50. Keast, D., and Walters, M.N.I.: *Immunology, 15:*247, 1968.
51. Keast, D.: *Immunology, 15:*237, 1968.
52. Teague, P.O., and Friou, G.J.: *Arthritis Rheum, 8:*474, 1964.
53. Teague, P.O., and Friou, G.J.: Submitted to *Immunology.*
54. Wolf, N.S., and Trentin, J.J.: *J Exp Med, 127:*205-214, 1968.
55. Stutman, O., Good, R.A., and Yunis, E.J.: *Fed Proc, 28:*376, 1969.
56. Kretschner, R., Janeway, C.A., and Rosen, F.S.: *Pediat Res, 2:*7, 1968.
57. Kretschner, R., August, C.S., Rosen, F.S., and Janeway, C.A.: *New Eng J Med, 281:*285, 1969.
58. Mellors, R.C., and Huang, C.Y.: *J Exp Med, 124:*1031-1038, 1966.
59. East, J., de Sousa, M.A.B., Prosser, P.P., and Jaquet, H.: *Clin Exp Immun, 2:*427-443, 1967.

60. Mellors, R.C., and Huang, C.Y.: *J Exp Med, 126*:53-62, 1967.
61. Mellors, R.C., Aoki, T., and Huebner, R.J.: *J Exp Med, 129*:1045-1062, 1968.
62. Tonietti, G., Oldstone, M.B., and Dixon, F.J.: *J Exp Med* (in press).
63. Stutman, O., Yunis, E.J., and Good, R.A.: *Exp Hemat, 16*:18-21, 1968.
64. Trainin, N., and Resnitzky, P.: *Nature, 221*:1154-1155, 1969.
65. Heremans, J.F., and Crabbe, P.A.: In Good, R.A., and Bergsma, D. (Eds.): *Immunologic Deficiency Diseases in Man.* Birth Defects Original Article Series. New York, The National Foundation Press, 1968, vol. 4, no. 1, p. 298.
66. Good, R.A., and Gabrielson, A.E.: In Wicks, J. (Ed.): *The Streptococcus, Rheumatic Fever and Glomerulonephritis.* Baltimore, The Williams Co., 1964, p. 368.
67. Cassidy, J.T., Burt, A., Sullivan, D.B., and Dickenson, D.G.: *Arthritis Rheum, 9*:850, 1966.
68. Cassidy, J.T., and Burt, A.: *Univ Mich Med Bull,* Nov.-Dec., 1968.
69. Bachman, R.: *Scand J Clin Lab Invest, 17*:316, 1965.
70. Amman, A.J., and Hong, R.: *J Lab Clin Med, 74*:846, 1969.
71. Huntley, C.C., Thorpe, D.P., Lyerly, A.D., and Kelsey, N.M.: *Amer J Dis Child, 113*:411-418, 1967.
72. Blajchman, M.A., Dacie, J.V., Hobbs, R., Jr., and Pettit, J.E.: *Lancet, 2*:340-344, 1969.
73. Alford, R.H.: *J Immun, 101*:984, 1968.
74. Perkins, J.C., Tucker, D.N., Knopf, H.L.S., Wenzel, R.P., Hormick, R.B., Kapikian, A.Z., and Chanock, M.M.: *Amer J Epidem, 90*:319, 1969.
75. Perkins, J.C., Tucker, D.N., Knopf, H.L.S., Wenzel, R.P., Kapikian, A.Z., and Chanock, R.M.: *Amer J Epidem* (in press).
76. Ogra, P.O., and Karrow, D.T.: *J Immun, 102*:15, 1969.
77. Mills, J., Knopf, H.L.S., van Kirk. J.E., and Chanock, R.M.: *Symposium on Local Antibody System.* Vero Beach, Florida, Dec. 10-13, 1969.
78. Giannini, D., and Sloan, R.S.: *Lancet, i*:525, 1957.
79. Cammarata, R.J., Rodnan, G.P., and Fennell, R.H.: *JAMA, 199*:455, 1967.
80. Burnet, M.: *The Clonal Selection Theory of Acquired Immunity.* Nashville, Vanderbilt University Press, 1958.
81. Walford, R.L.: *The Immunologic Theory of Aging.* Copenhagen, Munksgaard Press, 1969.

Chapter 5

MONOCLONAL AUTOANTIBODIES *

HENRY METZGER

I<small>N</small> A book on tolerance and autoimmunity it seems appropriate to discuss the interesting phenomena of monoclonal autoantibodies. At one end of the spectrum are those proteins which are present in only very low amounts and which, except for their apparent homogeneity, are indistinguishable from "ordinary" autoantibodies. At the other end of the spectrum are those monoclonal proteins arising in the course of clear-cut myelomatosis or Waldenstrom's macroglobulinemia. In these cases the proteins are present in very high concentrations, and it is the neoplastic rather than the autoimmune aspects of the disease which predominate.

My purpose is to review some examples of such autoantibodies to assess to what extent they are truly antibodies, and to suggest some directions for future research.

We recently had the opportunity to study intensively such an autoantibody, γM_{Lay},[1-4] a protein with rheumatoid factor-like activity which arose in an otherwise unremarkable case of Waldenström's macroglobulinemia. Our results allow us to give some reasonable answers to the questions of whether this protein is an antibody and indeed whether it is an autoantibody.

An antibody can be defined in several ways—the immunochemist stresses the molecular aspects; the cell biologist, the physiological ones. Both are relevant.

The gross structure of immunoglobulins is now well known.[5] Two pairs of heavy and light chains are joined to form a basic four-chain subunit. In γA and γM immunoglobulins, such subunits are linked to form higher polymers. Immunoglobulins are divided into

*From the Arthritis and Rheumatism Branch, National Institute Arthritis and Metabolic Diseases, National Institutes of Health, Bethesda, Maryland, 20014.

classes on the basis of long stretches of amino acid sequences which are common to all the proteins in a particular class. Antigen binding activity resides in specialized amino-terminal regions of both heavy and light chains where the sequences are highly variable for proteins within a particular class. There is one such region for each heavy-light chain pair.

We can therefore make certain predictions as to the number and location of combining sites to be expected for a particular immunoglobulin. Moreover, we have a large amount of data on binding constants, size of combining sites, specificity of those sites, etc., for conventional antibodies. In other words, we have functional and structural criteria by which to judge whether the binding of a particular material by an immunoglobulin represents an antibody-antigen interaction or some other less well defined binding phenomena.

By these criteria the protein γM_{Lay} is unquestionably an antibody. It is an intact γM immunoglobulin which reacts specifically with human and higher primate γG immunoglobulins, but with no other human serum proteins nor with γG immunoglobulins from lower primates or other mammals.[1] The combining sites are in the appropriate location within the molecule, the Fab regions,[1,2] and there is precisely one combining site for each heavy-light chain pair.[2,3] The binding constant is in the range of conventionally induced antibodies, and the thermodynamic constants associated with binding are not unusual.[3] Some of the properties which at first glance appeared to be unusual—the sensitivity of the precipitation to temperature, pH, and ionic strength—proved to be easily rationalized when studied more intensively.[3] (We often forget how much of our immunochemical experience is based on studies with heterogeneous γG antibodies. It should not surprise us, therefore, that in dealing with immunoglobulins of other classes—particularly with populations of antibodies having a single type of combining site—some of the phenomonology should change).

It is more difficult to decide whether a protein meets the physiologic criteria for an antibody. What do we really mean here? I think we can all agree that the following scheme is consistent with most of the data on the immune response and can be readily integrated into present concepts of cellular and molecular biology:

We envision an antibody precursor cell containing sufficient genetic information to produce at least one kind of immunoglobulin. This immunoglobulin acts as a receptor on the surface of the cell.[6] If the receptor is triggered by an antigen (leaving aside questions concerning the manner in which antigen may have to be presented to accomplish the task), the cell will differentiate into a cell capable of secreting antibodies and/or proliferate forming antibody secreting daughter cells. An antibody can then be defined as an immunoglobulin whose synthesis and secretion were, at least initially, stimulated by such antigen triggered differentiation. With respect to the proteins like γM_{Lay} we of course do not have historical data to say that this is what happened. We must rely on the activity of the protein and of others like it to provide clues as to its origin. Here the extraordinary specificity of γM_{Lay} is of some help.

Figure 5-1 illustrates current information on the evolution of the primates. By each major subdivision I have noted the degree of reactivity of the γG from representative animals with γM_{Lay}. It is clear that γM_{Lay} is reactive only with those γG's most closely related to human γG. Reactions with γG from lower primates and from other mammalian and nonmammalian species (dog, cat, sheep, horse, goat, mouse, rat, rabbit, and chicken) were insignificant.[4]

Other examples of proteins such as γM_{Lay} have been published.[7-11] Although specificity testing has usually been more cursory, the data show quite clearly that the primary specificity is for human γG. In addition to this striking autospecificity, the high incidence

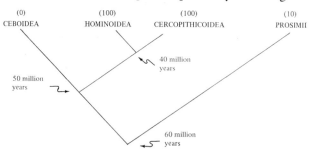

Figure 5-1. Comparison between evolutionary relationship of primates and the reactivity of their γG with γM_{Lay}. Degree of cross-reactivity is given in parentheses. Approximate time of divergence of species is indicated at the branch points.

of this kind of activity among Waldenström macroglobulins is remarkable. The incidence may be as high as 10 to 20 percent[12,13] although a rigorous systematic survey has not been made. These data are the most convincing evidence that we are not simply looking at the product of some clone of precursor cells which was randomly transformed into a neoplastic population and which began secreting a random antibody. The data suggest, rather, that a previously differentiated cell, already producing an antihuman γG, was induced to proliferate wildly.

While the most common autoantibody activity so far discovered among M components is antihuman γG activity, it is by no means the only one.[13] Another common one is that directed against the I antigen on human erythrocytes. This activity has been seen multiple times,[14,15] and the preferential tendency of such macroglobulins to cause agglutination of red cells in the cold produces clinical symptoms which may be the presenting complaint in such patients. These monoclonal antibodies are almost exclusively macroglobulins. γG and γA myelomas on the other hand are the ones most often associated with autoantibody activities resulting in a variety of aberrations in lipid metabolism.[16-21] Although none of these proteins has been extensively investigated with respect either to specificity or to the stoichiometry of the antibody reaction, there is every reason to believe that these are bona fide autoantibodies.

Coagulation disorders are common in myeloma, and in some cases at least there has been sufficient documentation to implicate directly the paraprotein. A variety of mechanisms may be involved, though a common mechanism appears to be some interference with fibrin monomer-polymer conversion.[22,23]

Some recent data on the binding activity of several induced myeloma proteins are instructive. They underline the difficulties in trying to reconstruct pathogenetic mechanisms from the apparent activity of a myeloma protein. Six mouse γA myeloma proteins, all of which precipitate with the C-polysaccharide of pneumococci, have been reexamined by Leon and Young.[24] They have now found that each of these will react with phosphorylcholine or its analogues. Two of the proteins have a spectrum of activity which is virtually identical. The others show distinctive patterns when reactions with choline, phosphorylcholine, phosphonocholine, and glycerophosphorylcholine are compared. Of particular interest is the observation that one of these γA proteins forms complexes with human β-lipoproteins and agglutinates erythrocytes sensitized with β-lipoproteins.

Here then we have an instance of several paraproteins whose binding activity was discovered only after extensive screening with a wide assortment of materials. The initially discovered activity appeared to be against a bacterial product—suggesting that perhaps a cell which had differentiated under the influence of an extrinsic antigen had undergone neoplastic transformation. After further examination, it now appears that these proteins could, after all, have autospecificity. What is particularly provocative is that the activities expressed by these mouse γA proteins are at least nominally similar to the activities of two human γA myelomas which have been studied by Beaumont and associates.[16,17]

Another set of immunoglobulins whose functions remains unexplained are the monoclonal (and more frequently polyclonal) immunoglobulins which are present in increased amounts in the sera of elderly individuals without known disease. Are these also antibodies?

Relatively little chemical work has been done on these proteins. All that one can say is that their gross characteristics (sedimentation constant, presence of heavy and light chains, presence of light and heavy chain genetic markers) are consistent with their being normal immunoglobulins.

Such "benign" serum M-components have recently been examined for evidence of antigen binding activity by Williams *et al.*[25] One hundred and five isolated human M-components were tested by gel diffusion against extracts from a variety of enteric bacteria, pneumococci, streptococci, and mycoplasma. No precipitin reactions were observed. Twenty of the M-components were examined by immunofluorescence for direct binding to cryostat sections of normal human lung, liver, kidney, and colon. No fluorescence above background was seen. Of considerable interest, however, was the observation that in several patients with carcinomas the tumor was heavily infiltrated with plasma cells filled with (and only with) the monoclonal M component observed in these patients' serums. In at least two instances a fluorescent antiserum made specific for the M component was said to show considerable staining of the tumor cell membranes, but *not* of cell membranes from adjacent normal tissues. It was not possible, however, to demonstrate reactivity between tumor antigens and the M components directly. These studies do not provide conclusive evidence for antibody activity among benign M-components. There are, however, a sufficient number of positive findings to make further exploration of such patients of interest.

CONCLUSIONS

I have reviewed the data on the binding properties of those monoclonal immunoglobulins which arise in the course of myelomatosis, Waldenström's macroglobulinemia, and normal aging. What data we have are consistent with the proposition that these proteins are intact immunoglobulins which bind ligands via combining sites indistinguishable from the combining sites on conventionally induced antibodies. Certain activities have been seen repeatedly. Many are clearly directed against self-antigens. Those that at first examination do not appear to be directed against self-antigens (i.e. those with either no known activity or with activities towards irrelevant antigens [nitrophenyl groups[26-30]] or extrinsic antigens [streptolysin[13, 32] or other bacterial components[33]]) may eventually be recognized as having autospecificity. These functional data suggest that the proteins are synthesized in cells stimulated by specific antigens.

It is not known why clones of autoantibody producing cells are stimulated during aging nor whether such autostimulated clones are particularly sensitive to neoplastic transformation. Further clarification of the binding properties of these proteins may provide clues which will eventually lead us to the answers to these questions.

REFERENCES

1. Metzger, H.: *Proc Nat Acad Sci*, 57:1490, 1967.
2. Stone, M.J., and Metzger, H.: *Cold Spring Harbor Symposium, Quant Biol*, 32:83, 1967.
3. Stone, M.J., and Metzger, H.: *J Biol Chem*, 243:5977, 1968.
4. Stone, M.J., and Metzger, H.: *J Immun*, 102:222, 1969.
5. Edelman, G.E., and Gall, W.E.: *Ann Rev Biochem*, 38:415, 1969.

6. Metzger, H.: *Ann Rev Biochem* 39:889, 1970.
7. Kirtzman, J., Kunkel, H.G., McCarty, J., and Mellors, R.C.: *J Lab Clin Med*, 57:905, 1961.
8. Grey, H.M., Kohler, P.F., Terry, W.D., and Franklin, E.C.: *J Clin Invest*, 47:1875, 1968.
9. Heimer, R., and Nosenzo, C.J.: *J Immunol*, 94:502, 1965.
10. Curtain, C.C., Baumgarten, A., and Pye, J.: *Arch Biochem Biophys*, 112:37, 1965.
11. Hannestad, K., *Clin Exp Immun*, 4-555, 1969.
12. Dammacco, F., Tursi, A., Bonomol, L.: *Haematologica*, 51:73, 1966.
13. Metzger, H.: *Am J Med*, 47:837, 1969.
14. Fudenberg, H.H., and Kunkel, H.G.: *J Exp Med*, 106:689, 1957.
15. Harboe, M.: *Proceedings of the 10th International Congress of Hematology*. Stockholm, Munksgaard, 1965.
16. Beaumont, J.L., Jocotot, B., Vilain, C., and Beaumont, V.: *CR Acad Sci*, 260:5960, 1965.
17. Beaumont, J.L.: *Comp Rend Sci Natur*, 269:107, 1969.
18. Feiwel, M.: *Brit J Derm*, 80:719, 1968.
19. Aubert, L., Arroyo, H., Detolle, P., Picard, D., and Cotte, G.: *Sem. Hop Paris*, 43:3014, 1967.
20. Spikes, J.L., Jr., Cohen, L., and Djordjevich, J.: *Clin Chim Acta*, 20:413, 1968.
21. James, W., Harland, W.R.: *Trans Amer Clin Climat Assn*, 79:115, 1968.
22. Krick, J.A., and Menache, D.: *Nouv Rev Franc Hemat*, 6:744, 1966.
23. Praga, C., Jean, G., and Cortellaro, M.: *Nouv Rev Franc Hemat*, 7:353, 1967.
24. Leon, M.A., and Young, N.M.: *Fed Proc*, 29:437, 1970.
25. Williams, R.C., Bailey, R.C., and Howe, R.B.: *Amer J Med Sci*, 257:275, 1969.
26. Eisen, H.N., Little, J.R., Osterland, C.K., and Simms, E.S.: *Cold Spring Harbor Symposium, Quantitative Biology*, 32:75, 1967.
27. Ashman, R.F., and Metzger, H.J.: *Biol Chem*, 244:3405, 1969.
28. Terry, W.D., Ashman, R.F., and Metzger, H.: *Immunochemistry*, 7:257, 1970.
29. Eisen, H.N., Simms, E.S., and Potter, M.: *Biochemistry*, 7:4126, 1968.
30. Jaffe, B.M., Eisen, H.N., Simms, E.S., and Potter, M.J.: *J Immun*, 103:872, 1969.
31. Zettervall, O.: *Acta Med Scand*, 184 (Suppl):492, 1968.
32. Seligmann, M., Danon, F., Basch, A., and Bernard, J.: *Nature*, 220:711, 1968.
33. Potter, M.: *Fed Proc*, 29:85, 1970.

Chapter 6

IMMUNOLOGICAL HYPERACTIVITY IN NEW ZEALAND MICE

NORMAN TALAL, ALFRED D. STEINBERG, AND PARKER J. STAPLES

NEW Zealand mice spontaneously develop, after three to four months of age, an autoimmune disease resembling human systemic lupus erythematosus. The major clinical features are an immune complex type glomerulonephritis, Coomb's positive hemolytic anemia, antibodies to nuclear components.[1] These mice carry murine leukemia virus and make antibodies to viral antigen. Genetic, immunologic, and viral factors are involved in the pathogenesis of this disorder.

Several laboratories have studied the immunologic reactions of New Zealand mice and found them to differ from control strains. The immunologic properties of New Zealand mice are highly age dependent and change depending on the stage of disease. For the first three months of life, the mice are clinically normal and show excessive antibody responses to certain antigens, such as bovine and human gamma globulin, bovine serum albumin, and sheep erythrocytes. They are relatively resistant to the induction of immunologic tolerance to ultracentrifuged bovine gamma globulin (BGG).[2] By contrast, during the first three weeks of life, New Zealand mice can be made tolerant to BGG. This tolerance, however, is lost within two to four weeks after challenge with BGG in Freund's adjuvant. Age and sex matched control strains (C3H, Balb/c, C57BL), made tolerant to ultracentrifuged BGG in the same way, retain their specific unresponsiveness for months.

This age difference in response to tolerogenic BGG made it possible to study different aged cell populations transplanted into irradiated syngeneic hosts.[3] In the following experiments, the recipients were thymectomized, lethally irradiated three-month old NZB/NZW F₁ mice. The donors were either two-week (young) or three-month (older)-old NZB/NZW F₁ mice. Ultracentrifuged BGG (10 mg) was injected intraperitoneally into the recipients on the day following cell transfer in an attempt at tolerance induction. Twelve days later, the recipients were challenged with BGG in Freund's adjuvant. According to their chronological age, the recipients would not be expected to develop tolerance. When repopulated with 18x10⁶ young spleen cells, the recipient mice became tolerant (Table 6-I). Control mice, repopulated with 18x10⁶ older spleen cells, did not become tolerant. The tolerance induced with young cells was transient, as is characteristic of young New Zealand mice.

TABLE 6-I

INDUCTION OF TOLERANCE TO BGG IN REPOPULATED
NEW ZEALAND MICE

Donor Cells	Tolerance Induced
Young Spleen	Yes
Older Spleen	No
Young Thymus and Young Bone Marrow	Yes
Older Thymus and Older Bone Marrow	No
Young Thymus and Older Bone Marrow	No
Older Thymus and Young Bone Marrow	Yes

In a second experiment, young and older thymus grafts and bone marrow cells were transplanted in place of spleen cells. When both thymus and bone marrow were from young mice, the recipients developed a transient state of tolerance, just as they did when young spleen cells were used. There was no tolerance when older thymus and bone marrow was grafted (Table 6-I).

In another part of this experiment, donor tissues were combined so that the thymus was of one age, and the bone marrow, another. When older bone marrow was used, the recipients failed to become tolerant, even in the presence of a young thymus. When young bone marrow was grafted, the recipients became tolerant, even in the presence of an older thymus (Table 6-I).

These experiments suggest that the bone marrow of New Zealand mice is of major importance in determining the response to tolerogenic BGG. Moreover, in the presence of the older thymus, the tolerance to BGG was of longer duration, and the rapid escape did not occur. This suggests that the older thymus may be relatively deficient in its ability to generate escape from tolerance. Indeed, tolerance was equally long when a heavily irradiated older thymus was used, suggesting that the older thymus may be hypofunctioning.

The concept of a relative thymic deficiency in New Zealand mice would also explain the failure of neonatal thymectomy to ameliorate their disease. Cellular immune functions, such as ability to induce a graft-versus-host reaction or reject tumor transplants, are prematurely impaired in New Zealand mice. These reactions depend upon a functioning thymus.

Our current concept is that an immunologic imbalance exists in New Zealand mice, with relative hyperactivity of bone marrow cells and antibody responses, and relative hypoactivity of the thymus and cellular reactions. How and why this should be are problems for further experimentation. The net result of this imbalance is the emergence of spontaneous autoimmunity, lymphoproliferation, and malignant lymphoma.

New Zealand mice, like human lupus patients, spontaneously produce antibodies that react with double stranded RNA and DNA.[4] The intraperitoneal administration of the synthetic double stranded RNA, polyinosinic polycytidylic acid (poly I· poly C), without carrier or adjuvant, immunizes New Zealand mice and accelerates the production of antinucleic acid antibodies. The effects of poly I·poly C in these mice is shown in Table 6-II. In spite of the induction of interferon, immune complex formation and glomerulonephritis are accelerated and the animals die prematurely.

TABLE 6-II

EFFECTS OF POLY I · POLY C IN FEMALE NZB/NZW F_1 MICE

Induction of interferon.
Induction of antibodies to RNA.
Induction of antibodies to DNA.
Deposition of RNA-containing immune complexes in the kidney.
Early death from glomerulonephritis.

These effects of poly I·poly C are specific. Other adjuvants, such as mineral oil or Corynebacteria parvum, do not induce antinucleic acid antibodies in New Zealand mice. Control strains of mice (C₃H, Balb/c, C₅₇BL) are not immunized by similar administration of poly I·poly C without adjuvant.

The spontaneous occurrence of antinucleic acid antibodies in murine and human lupus and the immunogenic properties of poly I·poly C in New Zealand mice, led us to propose that immunization to naturally occurring nucleic acids occurs with unusual ease in lupus.[4] We suggested that New Zealand mice, and by analogy lupus patients, were uniquely susceptible to immunization with nucleic acid antigens. The source of these immunogenic nucleic acids might be viral or mammalian. The role of viruses in the pathogenesis of lupus is particularly intriguing. New Zealand mice produce antibodies to murine leukemia virus,[5] but also show accelerated disease when infected with lymphocytic chorimeningitis or polyoma virus. Viral-like particles have recently been described in the tissues of lupus patients.[6]

Several models of latent viral diseases exist in animals and man. The role of the measles virus in the pathogenesis of subacute sclerosing panencephalitis has recently been explored. In lupus, the precise contribution of genetic, viral, and immunologic factors to pathogenesis is still obscure.

Since antibodies to nucleic acids appear to be important in the pathogenesis of murine and human lupus, we have for some time considered the induction of specific immunological tolerance to prevent their formation. The finding that poly I·poly C acts as a specific inducer of antinucleic acid antibodies made it possible to pursue these therapeutic concepts.

The administration of cyclophosphamide twenty-four hours after antigen leads to a state of specific immunologic tolerance, apparently by destroying rapidly proliferating sensitized cells. Animals so treated show a diminished response to subsequent antigenic challenge. We treated a group of one-month-old B/W female mice with two or three courses of poly I·poly C followed on the next day by cyclophosphamide. The mice were challenged with poly I·poly C in complete Freund's adjuvant and were bled two weeks later for assay of anti-RNA antibodies.

Animals that received poly I·poly C and cyclophosphamide made no detectable antibody to poly I·poly C following challenge. By contrast, animals treated with either poly I˙poly C alone or with cyclophosphamide alone were immunized by the challenge. Thus, the combined use of poly I˙poly C and cyclophosphamide in this schedule led to a profound state of immunologic tolerance. Animals made tolerant to poly I˙poly C responded normally to immunization with sheep erythrocytes demonstrating the specificity of the tolerance to poly I˙poly C.

We next treated a group of one-month-old B/W females with poly I˙poly C and cyclophosphamide, and instead of challenging them with antigen in adjuvant, we measured the spontaneous formation of antibodies to RNA. These were found to be significantly lower than in control mice treated with cyclophosphamide alone.

Recently we treated a group of six-month to seven-month-old B/W females already ill with glomerulonephritis and producing antibodies to nucleic acid. Mice treated with poly I˙poly C plus cyclophosphamide had a marked reduction in antibodies to both RNA and DNA as compared with controls treated with cyclophosphamide alone.

Sufficient reduction of antinucleic acid antibodies should theoretically result in decreased formation of circulating immune complexes. Other polynucleotides, in addition to or in place of poly I˙poly C, might be more effective in reducing anti-DNA antibodies. Our hope is that this therapeutic approach will be effective against the renal manifestations of lupus, will prove applicable to humans, and will be less toxic than continuous immunosuppression.

REFERENCES

1. Howie, J.B., and Helyer, B.J.: In Dixon, F.S., and Kunkel, H.G. (Eds.): *Advances in Immunology.* New York, Academic Press, 1968, Vol 9, p. 215.
2. Staples, P.J., and Talal, N.: *J Exp Med, 129:*123, 1969
3. Staples, P.J., Steinberg, A.D., and Talal, N.: *J Exp Med 131:*1223, 1970.
4. Steinberg, A.D., Baron, S., and Talal, N.: *Proc Nat Acad Sci 63:*1102, 1969.
5. Mellors, R.C., Aoki, T., and Huebner, R. J.:*J Exp Med, 129:*1045, 1969.
6. Norton, W.L., *J Lab Clin Med,* 74:369, 1969.

Chapter 7

VIRUS-INDUCED AUTOIMMUNITY AND THE AGING PROCESS

JOHN E. HOTCHIN

INTRODUCTION

THE idea that old age as we know it might be the result of virus infection seems at first sight to be a fantastic concept. This paper will attempt to show that there is evidence which suggests that premature senescence may be induced by the slow immunological rejection of host tissue infected months or years previously by a relatively harmless virus infection.

Most of the observations leading to this hypothesis stem from work on lymphocytic choriomeningitis (LCM) virus infection of mice. This combination makes a particularly interesting model since infection of the adult induces a rapidly fatal acute illness, while inoculation of the newborn, or congenital infection, induces a state of immunological tolerance to the virus with lifelong persistent infection. Study of these two states has revealed[1] two different pathogenic mechanisms. The persistent tolerant infection (PTI) confers almost complete immunological tolerance to the virus, but the acute disease takes the form of a violent homograft rejection of the infected cells by the host; this causes severe illness and extensive cellular necrosis which is usually fatal. In 1949 Burnet and Fenner[2] used the original observations of Traub[3, 4, 5] on LCM infection of mice, to propose the first concept of immunological tolerance which led to the wider view of acquired immunological tolerance developed by Medawar and his co-workers.[6]

It may be appropriate that the same LCM model should now be the basis of a hypothesis of virus-induced autoimmune aging.

132

THE LCM PERSISTENT INFECTION MODEL

Inoculation of Newborn Mice

The essentials of the PTI state will be briefly summarized here since this concept is basic to the theory of virus-induced aging. Neonatal or congenital LCM infection causes rapidly rising titers of virus throughout the animal in the few days immediately following infection. These titers remain very high throughout the lifespan of the animal, which averages about two-thirds that of uninoculated controls. During this period, chronic glomerulonephritis develops, and clinical signs of a late onset disease begin at seven to ten months of age in most mouse strains. Affected mice show ruffled fur, blepharitis, and a hunched posture. After a few months degenerative skin changes and marked hair loss develop, and the mice have an aged, dilapidated appearance.[1, 7] Typical

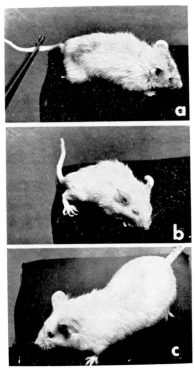

Figure 7-1a. Sixteen-month-old male PTI mouse; b—sixteen-month-old female PTI mouse; c—sixteen-month-old mouse inoculated with normal mouse liver.

PTI mice twenty-one months after infection are shown in Figure 7-1 a, b, and c with an uninoculated control mouse of the same age, c. It is of some interest that in his early work Traub remarked that several mice with congenital LCM infection began at ten months to show signs of old age, such as lack of liveliness, adiposis, and ruffled fur. In this laboratory LCM-PTI mice consistently weighed less than controls (Fig. 7-2) and after ten months began to die at an accelerated rate (Fig. 7-3). The level of their viremia tended to fall, and although no humoral antibody could be found by ordinary tests (complement-fixation [CF] and neutralization), low levels of antibody (titers of 1/8 to 1/16) were detected up to twelve months after infection by the indirect fluorescent antibody (FAB) technic using LCM-infected BHK cells as antigen.[8] Initially this antibody was maternal in origin, but the titers were maintained after maternal antibody had disappeared. The virological picture is summarized in Figure 7-4. An accelerated form of late disease was produced in one individual of parabiotically joined pairs of mice[1] when each pair consisted of one PTI and one LCM-immune mouse of the same age, sex, and inbred strain. The affected animal was always the PTI mouse; the immune animal remained normal, but often showed low levels of viremia.[9] Although the obvious cause of death of long term LCM-PTI mice appears to be glomerulonephritis, they show many other forms of autoimmune pathology including chronic hepatitis[7] and arteritis.[10] There is also some evidence[11] of neuropathology in the form of increased astrocytosis.

PTI mice appeared to be more aggressive and irritable than normal uninoculated mice of the same age and sex kept under the same conditions. This behavioral change was investigated during a study of the effects of electric shock avoidance learning (ESAL) stress upon acute and persistent LCM infection.[12] In the course of the ESAL experiments the behavior[13] of forty 14-20 gm PTI mice was compared with that of forty uninoculated controls of the same age and sex. Shock avoidance was achieved if the mice ran to the opposite end of the ESAL cage after a warning light went on for five seconds prior to the electric shock. Five mice of each type were put into the ESAL cage together; none had been exposed to it before. The PTI mice had been marked with dye, and the first five mice to cross the cage after the stimulus were counted.

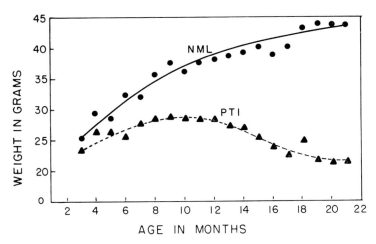

Figure 7-2. Average weight of control mice (inoculated neonatally with normal mouse liver [NML]) and PTI mice (inoculated neonatally with LCM virus).

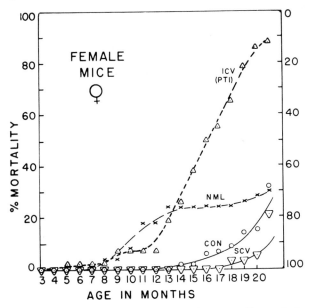

Figure 7-3. The relationship between cumulative mortality and time, in four groups of female mice. ICV = mice received LCM mouse liver IC at one day of age. NML = mice received normal mouse liver IC at one day of age. CON = mice received no inoculation. SCV = mice received LCM virus (same dose of ICV) at one month of age, by the SC route.

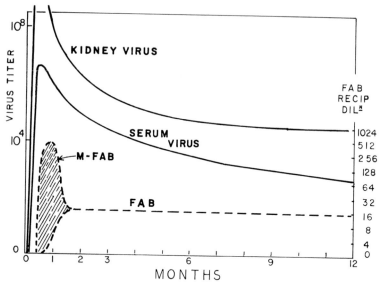

Figure 7-4. Diagram of the pathogenesis of persistent tolerant infection of mice with LCM virus. Studies of the FAB level in neonatal PTI mice revealed titers of 1/8 to 1/16 in animals tested up to twelve months after neonatal infection. M-FAB = maternal antibody, transferred via milk.

The scores of the two groups obtained in a typical experiment are shown in Table 7-I. Consistently comparable results were obtained

TABLE 7-I

SCORE OF PTI AND CONTROL MICE
COUNTING THE PROPORTION OF THE FIRST FIVE ANIMALS
TO RESPOND TO A WARNING STIMULUS IN THE ESAL BOX

Five mice of each type were placed together in the box at the same time.
(One set was marked.)

	Score Out of Five Mice	
Test No.	*PTI*	*Control*
1	3	2
2	4	1
3	3	2
4	3	2
5	3	2
6	5	–
7	4	1
8	3	2
Total	28	12

in repeated tests using different animals each time. In nine of ten cases the PTI mice scored higher than the controls (P = < 0.02), and PTI mice were the first to respond 70 percent of the time.

Inoculation of Adult Mice

The impression that PTI mice suffered premature aging stimulated further experiments with persistent LCM infection initiated in adult mice, since these animals showed the aged appearance but did not die from glomerulonephritis. Acute lethal disease does not occur when large doses of LCM virus are given to adult mice, particularly when the intravenous (IV) inoculation route is used; instead, a state of immune paralysis ensues, which in many ways resembles neonatal PTI. The adult persistent infection has been referred to in my laboratory as high dose immune paralysis (HDIP),[14] and this term will be used here. HDIP mice suppress their virus infection slowly, over a period of months; the rate of suppression is inversely proportional to initial virus dose and is somewhat more rapid in mice which are older at the time of inoculation. HDIP mice produce high titers of fluorescent, CF and finally neutralizing antibody; the general pattern of their virology is

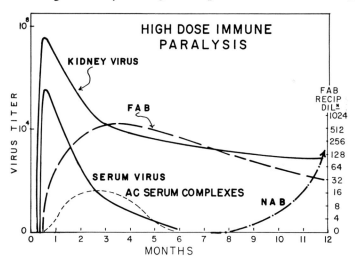

Figure 7-5. Diagram of the pathogenesis of the HDIP state following administration of large doses of viscerotropic LCM virus to the adult mouse via IC or IV inoculation. FAB=fluorescent antibody titer. NAB=neutralizing antibody titer. AC=anticomplementary.

shown in Figure 7-5. The animals exhibit "split tolerance" with a partial paralysis (with respect to LCM antigens) of cellular immunity but with no paralysis of active humoral antibody formation. The mice used in the experiments reported here received approximately 10^6 MID_{50} LCM virus IV at one month of age and had not suppressed viremia by one year after infection. The weight of the twenty-eight inoculated mice was consistently about 25 percent lower than that of the twenty uninoculated controls (Fig. 7-6), and their age/mortality curve showed a sharp rise in mortality after about the seventeenth month (Fig. 7-7).

As they became older, the HDIP mice showed evidence of hyperactivity with more running, jumping, and head movement than controls. Some of them exhibited periodic circling which became very rapid when they were illuminated by very bright lights for photography). The hyperactivity was measured in a modified open field test in which the mice were placed singly in an empty

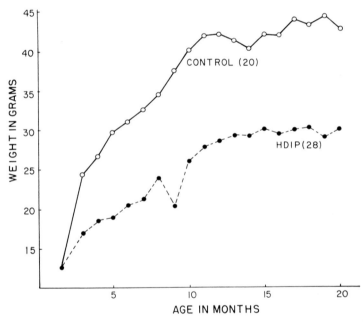

Figure 7-6. The effect of HDIP-LCM infection upon average mouse weight. Mice were inoculated IV with 10^6 MID_{50} LCM virus at one month of age. Control mice were inoculated with diluent only.

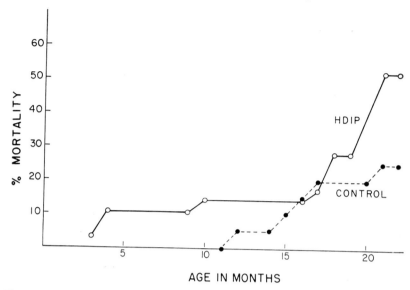

Figure 7-7. Cumulative mortality curves of mice used for Figure 7-6.

13-inch x 15-inch metal cage, the bottom of which had been divided into quarters by chalk lines. The number of lines crossed by each mouse was counted during the first and third minutes after placing the mouse alone in the cage. Ten randomly selected HDIP and control mice, aged twenty-two months, were individually evaluated with the results shown in Table 7-II. The HDIP mice were three times as active as the controls during the first minute

TABLE 7-II

ACTIVITY OF TWENTY-TWO-MONTH-OLD NORMAL CONTROL AND HDIP MICE IN A MODIFIED OPEN FIELD TEST*

Numbers refer to lines crossed during first and third minutes after placing individual mice in the test cage.

Type of Mouse		Lines Crossed During:	
		1st Minute	3rd Minute
Control	Total	354	164
	Average per mouse	7.08	3.3
HDIP	Total	1297	1077
	Average per mouse	25.9	21.5

*Ten mice from each group were tested on each of five different days. Results show the totals for all tests.

of testing; this difference was enhanced to a six-fold difference during the third minute.

LCM Virus-Induced Autoantibody in HDIP Mice

In an analysis of the different types of antiviral antibody found in HDIP mice, gel diffusion experiments using the Ouchterlony technic performed by Mr. E. Sikora in my laboratory revealed the presence of precipitating antibody when virus-infected tissue or tissue extracts were used as antigen. With tissue from certain organs, such as spleen or liver, at least two and sometimes three precipitin lines were present, as shown in Figure 7-8. When HDIP serum was reacted with LCM-infected liver, spleen, and kidney, a line of identity was obtained, common to all the tissues. No precipitin lines were present when the serum of normal mice was used. When normal tissue suspensions were used as controls, no lines were obtained with normal serum, but surprisingly, a definite precipitin line appeared between wells containing HDIP serum and normal spleen (see Fig. 7-8). Similar lines were obtained with

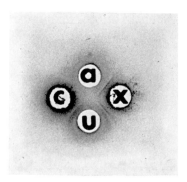

Figure 7-8. Precipitin lines in one percent agar (Colab #2) gel using phosphate buffered saline pH 7.6 with 7.5 percent glycine and 0.1 percent sodium azide. The center well contained HDIP serum from a two-month-old mouse.
X = LCM-infected liver tissue.
u = HDIP serum from a sixteen-month-old mouse.
c = Normal mouse liver tissue.
a = serum from a twenty-month-old breeder mouse which had been contact infected with LCM virus.
Two lines can be seen between the HDIP serum and virus-infected tissue, and one line, between it and normal tissue. The breeder serum shows only one line with the infected tissue.

normal liver, kidney, and brain tissue. Two separate lines were sometimes obtained with all of these except brain tissue, which gave only one line. One of the normal tissue lines showed identity between all the different normal tissues. When normal tissue was placed adjacent to LCM-infected tissue and reacted with HDIP serum, identity was established between one of the "normal" lines and one of the "LCM" lines. The detailed interrelationships of these antigens has yet to be worked out. It was concluded that the virus infection caused the production of antibody active against both LCM antigens and normal tissue components. Preliminary study of the time relationships of these antibodies showed them to be present from a few weeks after infection until at least twenty-two months of age.

Attempts were made to determine whether the antibodies reacted with viral and normal cell derived antigens in the cytoplasm or the cell membranes. These studies, performed by Miss L. Benson, utilized the indirect FAB technic. Using LCM-infected acetone-fixed, dried BHK cells as antigen, HDIP sera were shown to stain virus infected cells in a punctate, coarsely granular manner (Fig. 7-9A). Normal BHK cells were not stained. When suspensions of living cells were used, a fine ring of fluorescence resulted (Fig. 7-9B) indicating that both the cytoplasm and the cell membrane were involved in the reaction. There was no detectable visible difference between uninfected cells in a suspension and those which showed the ring fluorescence (see Fig. 7-9C). Neither infected nor normal cells were stained with normal control serum. When LCM-infected and control fixed strain L mouse tissue culture cells were used in a similar test, HDIP serum stained both normal and uninfected cells, but the granular virus antigen staining was only obtained with LCM-infected L cells. No staining of L cells occurred with normal mouse sera. These results confirmed the fact that the HDIP serum contained antibody reacting with a normal tissue antigen present in the cytoplasm; so far this antigen has not been detected on the cell surface.

The Mechanism of LCM Induced Autoimmunity

The present concept of LCM pathogenesis, based on work in this and several other laboratories has recently been reviewed[15] and

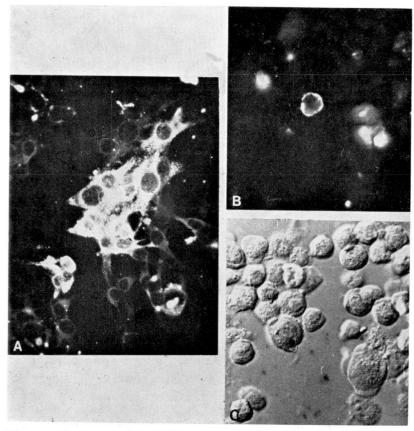

Figure 7-9A. Acetone-fixed LCM-infected BHK cells stained by the fluorescent antibody indirect method with anti-LCM human serum (convalescent) and antihuman FITC. The group of fluorescent cells shows granular fluorescence, which in the brightest areas appears homogenous in the photograph.

Figure 7-9B and 7-9C. LCM-infected BHK cells stained live (in suspension) by the fluorescent antibody indirect method with anti-LCM mouse serum and anti-mouse FITC. The same microscope field was photographed by: B: Fluorescence microscopy; C: Differential interference microscopy. Comparison of the two photographs shows the ring fluorescing cell is quite normal in appearance and cannot be distinguished from living controls. (Kindly photographed by Dr. Florian Muckenthaler, Department of Biology, State University of New York, Albany.)

is summarized diagrammatically in Figure 7-10. The virus infects most of the host cells, including many of the lymphoid cells, rendering them harmlessly, but persistently infected. In acute infec-

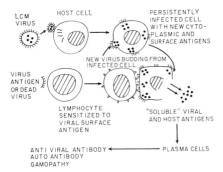

Figure 7-10. Diagram of pathogenic mechanisms of LCM virus infection.

tion of adults a massive cellular immune response occurs with generalized tissue rejection (similar to the homograft response and acute runt disease) which is usually fatal. In long-term persistent infection of the newborn (PTI) virtually all immune cells are persistently infected with virus, and immunological tolerance is almost complete. In HDIP infection of adults, a small portion of the cellular immune system escapes infection, and a chronic cellular immune attack upon the virus-infected cells ensues. This apparently results in the chronic liberation of cellular and viral antigens which escape into the circulation and cause chronic stimulation of the humoral antibody-forming system (plasma cells). This in turn results in the long-term production of high titers of antiviral and antinormal tissue antibodies, which may reach the proportions of a gamopathy. These antibodies are, however, unable to eradicate the persistent infection. The antibody which reacts with normal tissue may be made in response to liberated normal cellular constituents (not recognized as self), or may originate in response to the syntheis of a virus-modified cellular constituent. The latter type of antibody might well cross-react with normal cellular constituents in a manner analogous to the cross-reaction of antibody to a hapten + protein, with the original protein. This presupposes that the original protein (or other large molecule) is recognized as self and is therefore nonantigenic to the host animal.

The Effects of Neonatal Infection of Mice with Coxsackie Virus Upon Behavior and Aging

Coxsackie viruses A1 through A24 and B1 to B6 were each used to inoculate approximately eighty newborn mice. Several of

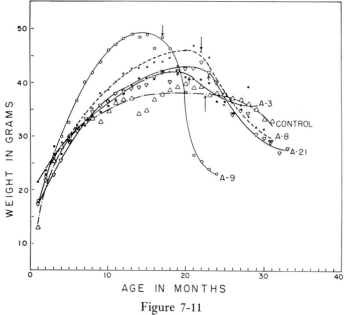

Figure 7-11

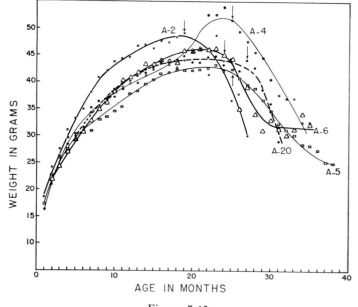

Figure 7-12

the viruses caused very high or complete mortality while others had little apparent effect. The cumulative, long-term mortality of the survivors was recorded, and the time for 50 percent mortality was calculated. For combined male and female mice this varied between twenty-three and thirty months in those groups which contained twenty or more total mice at the start of the experiment. The 50 percent mortality time for 115 control mice was nineteen months. There was no correlation between the acute mortality (death within one month of inoculation) and final (chronic) mortality, and all virus inoculated surviving groups showed extended life spans relative to the controls. Unfortunately in this experiment (which lasted for 3 years) only one group of controls was used. All animals were housed in the same room under identical conditions. The early mortality of the controls was due to fighting among the males.

When mortality was analyzed by sex, a clear-cut difference emerged between the control males and virus-inoculated males. The control males showed a much earlier 50 percent mortality time

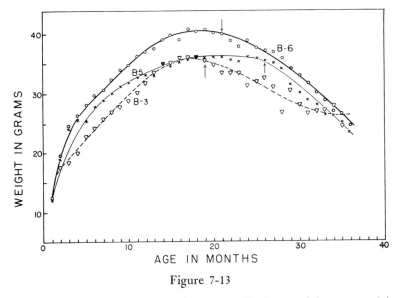

Figure 7-13

Figures 7-11, 7-12, and 7-13. Weight curves of mice surviving neonatal inoculation with Coxsackie viruses. Arrows show points of inversion of the slope of the curves used for Figure 7-14.

than females (11 months versus 31); however, this male/female difference was obliterated in the case of most of the groups of virus-inoculated survivors which generally showed little difference between male and female mortality. A total of 219 male and 269 female mice (survivors of 12 different virus infections) gave 50 percent mortality times of 24.5 and 26.3, respectively. The neonatal virus infection appeared to have exerted a feminizing effect in eliminating the normal male fighting and its accompanying mortality.

During the life span of the different virus-infected groups all mice were weighed at monthly intervals; the results were expressed as average weight per mouse, Figures 7-11—7-13. It was found that the time at which the slope of the weight curve became negative varied with different viruses. The shape of the curves was usually the same for both male and female infected mice. In the case of Coxsackie A-9 virus there was a particularly rapid initial growth rate followed by early and relatively rapid weight loss; this virus group also exhibited early mortality. The long-surviving animals of this group were noticeably more placid than controls, and the males appeared to be less irritable and less aggressive. The time when weight gain changed to loss was determined by inspection and is shown by small arrows on Figures 7-11—7-13. There appeared to be a direct relationship between mortality and the onset of weight loss; therefore the data were expressed as a graph (Fig. 7-14) relating age at 50 percent mortality to the time of inversion of the weight curve (the commencement of weight loss) for each virus group. Most of the points fall close to a straight line, indicating a correlation between beginning of weight loss and 50 percent mortality time. Two of the virus groups (male B-5 and female A-20) are considerably displaced from the line, but the male control group was the farthest point from the line in the whole series. An additional point was placed on Figure 7-14 from an experiment with a group of female mice neonatally inoculated with LCM virus. This additional point is close to the line on Figure 7-14, supporting the conclusion that the 50 percent mortality time is related to the time of commencement of weight loss, and that these factors can be varied as a result of virus infection in early life.

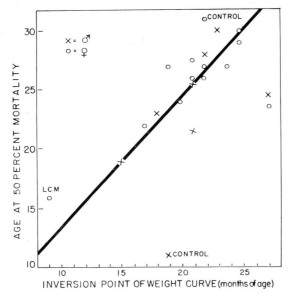

Figure 7-14. Relationship between age at 50 percent mortality and inversion point of weight curve of mice surviving neonatal inoculation with Coxsackie viruses. Each point represents one group of virus-infected or control mice.

No antibody studies were performed on these mice, since at the time of this study, the LCM antibody results had not been obtained.

Discussion

The main conclusion stemming from this work is that viruses may produce long-lasting subtle changes in young or adult mice which cause variations from the normal behavior and longevity. The long-term observation of the animals, particularly the mice with persistent LCM infection, conveys a powerful impression of virus-induced old age. More than thirty years ago the Pearls[16] suggested that the cause of aging was solely a genetic matter; since that time many other explanations have been offered. It is clear that the breakdown of key functions of many different types may lead to premature changes usually found only in old age. But old age is a very ill-defined clinical entity in spite of the fact that progeria can be clearly recognized, and many well-defined crippling metabolic or functional disabilities are not mistaken for premature old age.

Insulin insufficiency, vitamin and hormone deficiencies, anemias, inborn metabolic errors, psychoses, and many other definable conditions have their own clear-cut signs and symptoms without simulating senility. To a considerable extent, old age can be looked upon as a rather circumscribed disease entity, its precise cause remaining elusive.

Many different causes have been suggested, ranging from biochemical damage involving wear and tear of DNA molecules,[17] progressive cross linkage of long molecules,[18] cumulative effects of lysosome release,[19] and DNA polymerase activation,[20] to overabundant nutrition. The latter concept was based on early work[21] which showed that protein deprivation in early life increased longevity. Reduction of the body temperature of cold-blooded animals can also slow the rate of aging; this fact has been emphasized by Strehler[22] who calculated that lowering the body temperature of a man by 2 degrees C should increase life span by twenty years. Presumably there is an accelerative effect upon aging during fevers of infectious origin.

The Immune Response and Aging

An autoimmune cause of aging has been considered by several authors[23,24,25,26,27,28,29,30,31,32] and developed by Walford;[28] it has been reviewed by Ram.[33] All of the workers who have examined the autoimmune concept of aging appear to have looked to "spontaneous" events, such as genetic damage or the production of "forbidden clones" of immune cells, as a cause of the initial lesions. However, familiarity with molecular virology and perhaps more particularly with current trends in persistent viruses and slow viral disease provides a body of evidence that viruses are extremely powerful candidates for the induction of damage, previously believed to be genetic or autoimmune. Recent examples include the role of rubella virus in causing developmental defects and the multiple autoimmune lesions caused by the virus of Aleutian mink disease. There is a remarkable tendency for new, unexplained diseases to be considered genetic in origin and only later to be regarded as viral, when their infectious nature has been established beyond doubt. Kuru and scrapie, which will be discussed later, are excellent examples of this.

In general, immune function seems to decline in intensity with advancing age. In aged mice an increase was found[34] in the proportion of spleen cells capable of making autoimmune hemolytic antibody (demonstrated by the agar plaque technic). Aging phenomena have also been ascribed, in part, to depletion of immunocompetent cells. Both are made more severe by thymectomy in early life[35] and by chronic exposure to δ radiation. In advancing age, human lymphocyte response to phytohemagglutinin has been reported to decrease[36] and response to a new antigen (sensitivity to 2, 4-dinitrochlorobenzene) also diminished[37] although reactivity to tuberculin did not change.[37] No correlation appears to exist between the activity of cellular and humoral immunity. The RNA/DNA ratio of human peripheral blood lymphocytes was found[38] to rise with advanced age, approximating and then exceeding the high values usually associated in younger people with acute inflammatory disease. It is tempting to speculate that this might be associated with a late-developing autoimmune response. Walford[39, 40, 41] has emphasized the role of autoimmune phenomena in the aging process and proposed that aging is a consequence of increasing immunogenetic diversification of the dividing cell populations of the body.[28] He cites amyloidosis and maturity-onset diabetes as examples of autoimmune lesions which appear to be age-related and gives some evidence that parabiotically joined animals show premature aging. The mechanism may be similar to that of the parabiotic LCM-infected mice reported here. It may also be relevant that amyloid-like depositions[7] and arteritis[42] occur in LCM-PTI mice. A virus-induced adult diabetes has been produced in mice by Toolan[43] after neonatal inoculation of the H1 picodna virus.[44]

If the LCM-induced changes reported here can be regarded as a form of aging, the results appear to carry the autoimmune theory further in two respects. They establish additional experimental data linking chronic autoimmune tissue rejection with a clinical appearance of accelerated senescence and provide a causative agent in the form of a virus. However, objective criteria for true senility, such as soluble/insoluble collagen ratios are at present lacking. The autoimmune nature of the pathogenesis of this disease is now well established,[1, 15] and the virus is known to mature by inducing new antigens at the cell surface[45] where it reproduces by budding.[46] The finding of autoimmune antibodies in the serum of HDIP mice is believed to be the first report of experimental virus-induced anti-normal tissue antibody, and the association of this antibody with premature aging and behavioral changes should stimulate more investigation of this and related systems. The presence of precipitating autoantibodies in the LCM-infected mice may conceivably be related to the numerous observations of gammapathy in man during old age. Englïsová *et al.*[47] found electrophoretic evidence of increasing monoclonal gammapathy in humans of advanced ages. The antibrain and other tissue antibodies of LCM-HDIP mice appear to be similar to those found in spontaneous thyroiditis of chickens[48] and of man in Hashimoto's chronic thyroiditis. Svec and Viet[49] reported the presence in sera of aged women of antibodies to thyroid, parietal cell, skeletal muscle, and heart muscle. Sometimes, but not aways, the antibodies were organ specific. No correlation was found with clinically recognized diseases. As many as 36 percent of elderly persons have been reported[50] to have circulating antinuclear factor which could not be explained by the presence of rheumatic disease.[51] Similar findings in old people have been reported by others.[40, 41, 52, 53] It has been suggested[54] that mutations play a dominant role in the aging process, and Cammarata *et al.*[50] suggested that the antiglobulin and antinuclear factors represent antibodies to various new, immunologically foreign serum and tissue proteins. Litwin and Singer[55] have shown however that the anti-δ globulin factors in the elderly do not react with the known genetic sites on human δ globulin or the various anti-D human δ globulin coats on RBC's, indicating that these antibodies may not be true autoantibodies but may be specific for new or changed antigens, not normally found in the circulation. This conclusion is in keeping with the concept that some immunological changes in antigens responsible for aging phenomena may be induced by viruses.

Nonpersistent Neonatal Virus Infection

The results with Coxsackie viruses described here must be regarded as preliminary, since insufficient data are available for final evaluation of their significance. The original purpose of the experiments was a study of virus-induced neurological disease, and the results are included here since they appear to show that neonatal virus infection can influence the rate of aging. Neonatal infection of mice with several different members of the Coxsackie virus group can initiate subtle changes which affect the aggressiveness of male mice, and influence longevity, although there is no evidence that these viruses persist. The weight and mortality changes indicate a direct relationship between age at death and age when weight begins to be lost. This type of straight line relationship fits the equation $y = mx + k$, where $y =$ age at 50 percent death, $m = 1$ (slope), and $x =$ the age at inversion point. In this case (Fig. 7-14) k proves to be 6.5 months, so the age at 50 percent death turns out to be 6.5 months after the start of the weight loss process (inversion point). A similar relationship has been previously reported[56, 57] for aging animals. Conceivably this process can be triggered by a "slow" virus with a long incubation period, just as clinical neurological damage in scrapie-affected mice appears quite suddenly after an interval of many months (see below). Alternatively, the onset of weight loss may be an indicator of some "metabolic titration" which has at last reached an end point. Some of the Coxsackie viruses appeared to extend life span by diminishing or preventing male aggressive behavior. The mechanism of this effect is not at all clear and needs further experimentation. It is possible that thyroid function was affected, and basic metabolic rates need to be measured for these mice, HDIP mice, and appropriate controls. The finding that exposure of newborn mice to sex hormones[58, 59] affects their subsequent aggressive behavior after maturity, may be relevant to the apparent "feminizing" effect of neonatal Coxsackie virus infection described here. Very low levels of male sex hormone present in the neonatal male or female mice have been found [58] to sensitize or trigger the nervous system of the animal to react with aggressive behavior to subsequent mature levels of male hormone. Conversely brief neonatal treatment of male mice with female hormone prevents this sensitization, producing normal appearing male mice which do not behave aggressively after developing their mature levels of male hormone. The "feminizing" results described here may be the result of a similar mechanism, whereby neonatal virus infection temporarily inhibits or reduces the normal production of male hormone during the neonatal sensitizing phase. Future studies should attempt to test this hypothesis, which is strengthened by the ability of testicular tissue to support the growth of numerous viruses.

Virus infections may produce lesions at the biochemical or molecular level which ultimately cause sufficient damage to constitute overt disease. The end results of appropriate types of damage could be akin to premature aging. In this respect it might be profitable to consider one aspect of the problem of aging, by treating it as a potential slow virus disease, whether this is caused by autoimmune mechanisms or a direct effect of virus upon cells. The behavior of slow viruses has many interesting features which suggest a similar etiological mechanism to the aging process. Scrapie[60] and kuru,[61] fatal degenerative diseases of the nervous system of sheep and man, respectively, were both considered to be genetically caused[62, 63] before their viral nature[64, 65] was demonstrated. In the case of scrapie, the genetic view obstinately persisted as late as 1963[66] even though the infectious nature of the disease was demonstrated in 1938.[65] Both have incubation periods running into several years, followed by relatively sudden onset and rapid deterioration. The mechanism of damage with these viruses is at present quite unknown, and the unusual nature of the scrapie agent is emphasized by results which suggest that it may not contain nucleic acid[67] in spite of its ability to replicate. There is some similarity in the neuropathology of scrapie and that of very old mice.[68] Both show amyloid deposits in the brain and hypertrophy of astroglial cells, although these changes are much more extensive in the virus-infected animals than in aged controls. In these respects the changes of scrapie appear to be an exaggerated form of the neuropathology of old age. However, this may be a dangerously oversimplified conclusion. The mechanism and function of astroglial hypertrophy is unknown and may represent a compensatory host response to a foreign agent in the brain. If so, astroglial response would be expected to be stimulated both by scrapie virus and other viral agents responsible for slow subtle changes which cumulatively are presented as old age.

Slow virus-induced behavioral changes have been previously described; early phases of rabies infection classically cause extreme irritability and aggression in many mammalian species, and kuru is accompanied by behavioral changes prior to clinical disease in both man[69] and the chimpanzee, as is scrapie in mice.[70, 71] Subacute sclerosing panencephalitis also initially causes only behavioral changes, and there is mounting evidence that measles virus may be the cause of this fatal human disease.[72] These behavioral changes and those of mice with LCM autoimmune disease suggest that psychoses might be produced by the same mechanism. An autoimmune concept of manic depressive psychosis was proposed by Burch,[73] and a slow virus etiology for some long-term human behavioral changes appears to be quite likely. Lactic dehydrogenase elevating virus produces a long-term infection of mice in which the only marked change is persistent elevation of certain serum enzymes;[74] clearly, virus-induced long-term metabolic effects have already been recorded; no doubt many other comparable agents remain to be discovered.

Several other important slow virus diseases should be mentioned for their general relevance to virus-induced autoimmune and age-related diseases. Aleutian mink disease is due to a persistent virus[75] which causes multiple autoimmune lesions and a marked gammapathy.[76, 77] Equine infectious anemia is similar in many respects,[78, 79] and the virus can persist in the blood of affected animals for years.[80] Human serum hepatitis sometimes detected by the presence of Australian antigen can also persist for years[81, 82] and appears to sometimes induce a state of semipermanent immunological tolerance. African swine fever,[83] Machupo,[84] and visna[85] are also able to induce long-term persistence of the causative virus with little or no detectable immune response. The autoimmune aspects of those and other slow viruses have been recently reviewed.[15]

Persistent viruses may cause pathological effects in the total absence of an immune response. Kuru and scrapie initiate late onset pathological changes in a target organ (the brain) in spite of the fact that no evidence of any immune response whatever, in any animal, has been reported up to the present time, for these agents. Latent viruses of mice are so common that no known virus-free animal has yet been obtained. Mammary cancer and leukemia agents are ubiquitous, and Grünberg[86] has suggested that some differences between substrains of inbred mice may be due to carrier viruses rather than genetic differences. A mass of circumstantial evidence suggests that a similar situation holds for all complex life forms, including man. For example, King Edward VII potatoes all carry paracrincle virus.[87] Although these infected plants were regarded as normal, when freed of virus they were visibly different and gave a greater yield. We are far from obtaining virus-free mammals, and we live virologically in a milieu which is contaminated to an almost unbelievably heavy extent. Although acute illness has been controlled to a large extent during the past century, chronic disease is increasing and will increase at a rate approximately twenty percent faster than the population increase.[88] The chronic diseases are rapidly assuming a role of major importance. The slow and persistent viruses will probably be the major medical problem in a few years' time. Perhaps advances in biological technics, such as parthenogenetic reproduction, *in vitro* culture of mammalian embryos, and antiviral agents, will permit the attainment of virus-free strains of gnotobiotic animals. It will be interesting to see how long they live.

ACKNOWLEDGMENTS

The author wishes to acknowledge the help of Miss L. Benson and Mrs. M. Clark in the preparation of the manuscript. Grateful thanks are also expressed to Dr. Florian Muckenthaler of the Biology Department, State University of New York at Albany, who kindly performed the differential interference photomicrography.

REFERENCES

1. Hotchin, J.: *Cold Spring Harbor Symposium Quantitative Biology*, 27: 479, 1962.
2. Burnet, F.M., and Fenner, F.: *Monograph, Walter and Eliza Hall Institute*, 2nd ed. Melbourne, Macmillan and Co. Ltd., 1949.
3. Traub, E.: *Science*, *81*:298, 1935.
4. Traub, E.: *J Exp Med*, *63*:533, 1936.
5. Traub, E.: *J Exp Med*, *69*:801, 1939.
6. Billingham, R.E., Brent, L., and Medawar, P.B.: *Philos Trans Royal Soc Lond*, 239 *(Section B)*: 357, 1956.
7. Hotchin, J., and Collins, D.N.: *Nature*, *203*:1357, 1964.
8. Benson, L., and Hotchin, J.: *Nature*, *222*:1045, 1969.
9. Hotchin, J.: Slow, latent and temperate virus infections. *NINDB Monograph No. 2.* 1965, p. 341.
10. Pollard, M., Kajima, M., and Sharon, N.: *Perspectives in Virology*, New York, Academic Press, 1968, Vol. 6, p. 193.
11. Zlotnik, I., and Hotchin, J.: Unpublished observations.
12. Sikora, E., Benson, L., and Hotchin, J.: To be published.

13. Hotchin, J., and Sikora, E.: *Proc Soc Exp Biol Med*, in press, 1970.
14. Hotchin, J., and Benson, L.: *J Immun, 91*:460, 1963.
15. Hotchin, J.: *Proceedings of the 3rd International Symposium on Medical and Applied Virology.* In press.
16. Pearl, R., and Pearl, R.D.: *The Ancestry of the Long Lived.* Baltimore, Johns Hopkins Press, 1934.
17. Medvedev, Z.A.: In Shork, N.W. (Ed.): *Perspectives in Experimental Gerontology.* Springfield, 1966, p. 336.
18. Bjorksten, J.: *J Amer Geriat Soc, 6*:740, 1958.
19. DeDuve, C., Pressman, B.C., Gianetto, R., Wattiaux, R., and Appelmans, F.: *Biochem J, 60*:604, 1955.
20. Comfort, A.: *Lancet: ii*:1325, 1966.
21. Slonaker, J.R.: Amer J Physiol, *98*:266, 1931.
22. Strehler, B.L.: *Geront, 8*:14, 1968.
23. Burch, P.R.J.: *Lancet, ii*:299, 1963.
24. Burnet, F.M.: *The Clonal Selection Theory of Acquired Immunity.* Nashville, Vanderbilt University Press, 1959.
25. Comfort, A: *Lancet, ii*:138, 1963.
26. Comfort A.: *Progress in the Biological Sciences in Relation to Dermatology—2.* London, Cambridge University Press, 1964.
27. Comfort, A.: *Ageing, the Biology of Senescence*, 2nd ed. London, Routledge and Kegan Paul, 1964.
28. Walford, R.L.: *J Geront, 17*:281, 1962.
29. Blumenthal, H.T., and Berns, A.W.: In Strehler, B.L. (Ed): *Advances in Gerontological Research.* New York, Academic Press, 1964, Vol. 1.
30. Burnet, F.M.: *Brit Med J*, 2:645 and 720, 1959.
31. Comfort, A.: *Amer Heart J*, 62:293, 1961.
32. Comfort, A.: *The Process of Ageing.* London, Weidenfeld and Nicolson, 1965.
33. Ram, J.S.: *J Geront, 22*:92, 1967.
34. Hildemann, W.H., and Walford, R.L.: *Proc Soc Exp Biol Med, 123*:417, 1966.
35. Davis, W.E., Jr., and Cole, L.J.: *Exp Geront, 3*:9, 1968.
36. Westring, D.W., DePrey, C., Seaberg, F., and Pisciotta, A.V.: *Clin Res, 12*:345, 1964.
37. Waldorf, D.S., Wilkens, R.F., and Decker, J.L.: *JAMA, 203*:831, 1968.
38. Sakai, H., Kato, E., Matsuki, S., and Asano, S.: *Lancet: i*:818, 1968.
39. Walford, R.L.: Aspects of the biology of ageing. *Symposia of the Great Britain Society of Experimental Biology.* New York, Academic Press, 1967, vol 21, p. 351.
40. Walford, R.L.: *Advances in Gerontologic Research.* New York, Academic Press, 1967, vol. 2.
41. Walford, R.L.: *Exp Geront, 1*:67, 1964.
42. Pollard, M., and Sharon, N.: *Proc Soc Exp Biol Med, 132*:242, 1969.

43. Toolan, H.W.: Personal communication.
44. Toolan, H.W.: *International Review of Experimental Pathology.* New York, Academic Press, 1968, vol. 6, p. 135.
45. Abelson, H.T., Smith, G.H., Hoffman, H.A., and Rowe, W.P.: *J Nat Cancer Inst, 42*:497, 1969.
46. Dalton, A.J., Rowe, W.P., Smith, G.H., Wilsnack, R.E., and Pugh, W.E.: *J Virol, 2*:1465, 1968.
47. Englĭsová, M., Englis, M., Kyral, V., Kourílek, K., and Dvorák, K.: *Exp Geront, 3*:125, 1968.
48. Witebsky, E., Kite, J.H., Jr., Wick, G., and Cole, R.K.: *J Immun, 103*:708, 1969.
49. Svec, K.H., and Veit, B.C.: *J Lab Clin Med, 73*:378, 1969.
50. Cammarata, R.J., Rodnan, G.P., and Fennell, R.H.: *JAMA, 199*:455, 1967.
51. Lawrence, J.S.: *Arthritis Rheum, 6*:166, 1963.
52. Tuffanelli, D.L., *Brit J Vener Dis, 42*:40, 1966.
53. Whitaker, R.R., and Willken, R.F.: *Clin Res, 14*:143, 1966.
54. Curtis, H.J.: *Science, 141*:686, 1963.
55. Litwin, S.D., and Singer, J.M.: *Arthritis Rheum, 8*:538, 1965.
56. Everitt, A.V.: *J Geront, 12*:382, 1957.
57. Everitt, A.V.: *Geront, 2*:21, 1958.
58. Edwards, D.A.: *Science, 161*:1027, 1968.
59. Bronson, F.H., and Desjardins, C.: *Science, 161*:705, 1968.
60. Zlotnik, I., and Stamp, J.T.: *World Neurol, 2*:895, 1961.
61. Gajdusek, D.C., and Zigas, V.: *Amer J Med, 26*:442, 1959.
62. Report of the General Assembly of the United Nations: Administration of the territory of New Guinea July 1, 1963, to June 30, 1964. Canberra, Department of Territories 1964, chapter 4.
63. Stamp, J.T.: *Vet Rec, 70*:50, 1958.
64. Gajdusek, D.C., Gibbs, C.J., Jr., and Alpers, M.: *Nature, 209*:794, 1966.
65. Cuillé, J., and Chelle, P.L.: *CR Acad Sci, 206*:78, 1938.
66. Draper, G.J.: *Heredity, 18*:165, 1963.
67. Alper, T., Haig, D.A., and Clarke, M.C.: *Biochem Biophys Res Commun, 22*:278, 1966.
68. Field, E.J.: *Deutsch Z Nervenheilk, 192*:265, 1967.
69. Gajdusek, D.C., and Zigas, V.: *New Eng J Med, 257*:974, 1957.
70. Savage, R.D., and Field, E.J.: *Anim Behav, 13*:443, 1965.
71. Heitzman, R.J., and Corp, C.R.: *Res Vet Sci, 9*:600, 1968.
72. Zeman, W., and Kolar, O.: *Neurology, 18*:1, 1968.
73. Burch, P.R.J.: *Brit J Psychiat, 110*:808, 1964.
74. Mahay, B.W.J., Parr, C.W., and Rowson, K.E.K.: *Nature, 198*:885, 1963.
75. Porter, D.R., and Larsen, A.E.: *Proc Soc Exp Biol Med, 126*:680, 1967.
76. Gordon, D.A., Franklin, A E., and Karstad, L.: *Canad Med Assn J, 96*:1245, 1967.

77. Henson, J.B., Gorham, J.R., and Leader, R.W.: *Nature*, *197*:206, 1963.
78. Henson, J.B., McGuire, T.C., Kobayashi, K., and Gorham, J.R.: *J Amer Vet Med Assn*, *151*:1830, 1967.
79. Ishii, S.: *Advances Vet Sci*, *8*:263, 1963.
80. Stein, C.D., Mott, L.O., and Gates, D.W.: *J Amer Vet Med Assn*, *126*:277, 1955.
81. Blumberg, B.S., Melartin, L., Guinto, R.A., and Werner, B.: *Amer J Hum Genet*, *18*:594, 1966.
82. Zuckerman, A.J., and Taylor, P.E.: *Nature*, *223*:81, 1969.
83. Steyn, D.G.: *18th Rept. Director, Vet Serv Animal Ind Onderstepoort (South Africa)*, *1*:99, 1932.
84. Johnson, K.M., Wiebenga, N.H., Mackenzie, R.B., Kuns, M.L., Tauraso, N.M., Shelokov, A., Webb, P.A., Justines, G., and Beye, H.: *Proc Soc Exp Biol Med*, *118*:113, 1965.
85. Gudnadóttir, M., and Pálsson, P.A.: *J Immun*, *95*:1116, 1966.
86. Grünberg, H.: *Nature*, *225*:39, 1970.
87. Smith, K.M.: *Viruses*. London, Cambridge University Press, 1962, p. 95.
88. Traddle, A.C.: *J Chronic Dis*, *21*:417, 1968.

Chapter 8

IMMUNE CYTOLYSIS IN VIRAL INFECTIONS

MONROE D. EATON

MANY viral infections appear to have an autoimmune component causing at some stage of the disease immunological enhancement of the pathologic process. It is also suspected that infection with unknown viruses or perhaps vertically transmitted leukemia virus may play a part in the so-called spontaneous autoimmunity discussed in this book. We shall present some *in vitro* and *in vivo* models of immune cytolysis confirmatory of Dr. Hotchin's observations with L.C.M. but with different viruses and using tumor cells instead of the normal tissues of the mouse.

Autoimmunity has been described most frequently in chronic virus diseases, such as congenital L.C.M., scrapie, aleutian mink disease, and visna virus infection of sheep. Here the persistence of virus in the tissues is accompanied by production of antibodies and immune lymphocytes by the host. But complications of acute infections, especially those produced by paramyxoviruses, such as measles, mumps, and respiratory syncytral virus, may also have autoimmune components. The pathology may be demyelinating disease, inflammation of glandular tissues, glomerular nephritis, or monocytic reactions in the pulmonary parenchyma or bronchioles.

The pathologic reaction in all virus infections, acute or chronic, is characterized by lymphocytic infiltration of the infected tissues. The exact function of the "cuff" of lymphoid cells around a blood vessel or bronchiole is still somewhat of a mystery. It is generally assumed that at least some of these cells are forming antibody. It is also noteworthy that the cellular reaction occurring in the rejection of foreign tissue resembles quite closely that characteristic of virus infections. The question may be raised, therefore, as to whether or not the lymphoid cells, instead of forming antibody to neutralize the infecting virus, may, under some conditions, bring about destruction of virus-infected cells. An *in vitro* model for this can be found in the observations of Speel *et al.*[1] who demonstrated that splenocytes from animals immune to mumps virus partially destroyed cultures of human conjuctival epithelial cells chronically infected with that virus. Dr. Hotchin has just presented another example of the phenomenon with L.C.M.

There is no doubt that humoral antibody can cause antiviral immune cytolysis *in vitro* and sometimes *in vivo*. Recent observations with simian virus 5[2] indicate that differences in membrane composition of various cells may determine resistance or susceptibility apart from the amount of viral replication. Other examples of antibody mediated cytolysis have been described for rabies in tissue culture[3] and for two paramyxoviruses Newcastle disease (NDV) and Sendai[4] *in vitro*. With chronic L.C.M. infections in mice, administration of antibody results in acute inflamatory reactions probably anologous to those observed *in vitro*.[5] On the basis of antibody studies in newborns Chanock[6] has postulated that infection with respiratory syncytial virus may be complicated by immunologic enhancement because of an excess of circulating 7S maternal antibody and a deficiency of secretory IgA which in older individuals protects against infection in the lungs.

What is the primary antigen in autoimmunity associated with viral infections? It may be a constituent of normal tissue to which antibodies are developed through some poorly understood process in infection. Or it may be one of the structural antigens of the virus. A third possibility is that the virus specifies genetically neoantigens which are neither part of the virus particle nor found in normal tissue. These antigens occur in virus induced tumors and are not inconceivable as a product of nononcogenic viruses. In the case of myxoviruses, budding and antigenic transformations at the cell membrane have been extensively studied. Maturation and inclusion of viral RNA in the envelope is accompanied by the appearance of viral antigen at that site as demonstrated with ferritin labeled antibody against the purified virus. Ferritin labeled antibody to normal cell membrane reacts poorly or not at all at the site of viral maturation, but gives heavy deposits of ferritin at adjacent areas of the cell where virus is *not* budding through. In other studies it is found that the viral envelope may include lipids or polysaccharides from the host cell but very little host cell protein. The lipid composition of a paramyxovirus grown in various tissues varies to some extent. Therefore antibody to virus grown in the allantoic sac of chick embryos, for example, may be expected to show very little reaction with normal mouse tissue, and the reaction with budding virus may be attributed to the structural antigens of the virus. Appropriate controls can be set up with an antigenically unrelated myxovirus grown and tested in the same way.

Our observations were initiated with a transplantable ascites lymphoma induced in C_3H/Bi mice by the Gross leukemia virus. This lymphoma is highly malignant and uniformly fatal after inoculation of a few cells. Antigenicity in the syngeneic host is extremely low or nonexistent since repeated doses of maximum tolerated numbers of cells induced no significant transplantation immunity. Treatment of the lymphoma cells with NDV or Sendai virus in high virus/cell multiplicity before intraperitoneal injection into mice resulted in some inhibition of cell growth in the animal and larger doses of lymphoma were tolerated. We then considered the possibility that virus infection of the tumor cells might induce a state of autoimmunity in mice to the syngeneic tumor. It was found that repeated injection of virus-infected lymphoma cells did indeed increase resistance to transplantation of cells preinfected with virus,[7] but challenge of such virus-cell immune mice with untreated lymphoma cells showed that resistance was not significantly greater than that of normal mice. Finally it was found that immunization of mice with the virus alone produced essentially the same effect, and it was concluded that immunity to the structural antigens of the virus contributed to oncolysis *in vivo*.

To support this idea an *in vitro* model was developed. Ascites lymphoma cells were infected with NDV or Sendai virus in Eagle's Medium containing 2 percent bovine albumin and 50-250 HA units of virus. After an adsorption period of one hour cells were washed, resuspended in Eagle's Medium with 10 percent calf serum, and incubated in roller tubes for twelve to twenty hours. This period and input multiplicity were adjusted so that most cells would become infected but not yet killed as determined by dye exclusion. Cells were then washed and prepared for measurements of respiration in the Warburg apparatus. Antiviral antibody obtained by immunizing rabbits with NDV, Sendai, or influenza (PR$_8$) virus grown in the allantoic sac of chick embryos was added at a concentration of 25-100 hemagglutination-inhibiting units. Complement was used at 1:20 to 1:30 dilution of fresh normal guinea pig or normal rabbit serum. In addition to the PR$_8$ antiserum with NDV or Sendai-infected cells other controls were uninfected cells with antiviral serum and complement and infected cells with antiserum only.

The rate of O$_2$ consumption at hourly intervals is shown in Figure 8-1. The respiration of cells infected with Sendai declined much more rapidly in the presence of the related antiserum than with PR$_8$ antiserum. With the Sendai antiserum alone less rapid killing was observed than in the presence of complement. NDV by itself produced a more rapid viral cytopathic effect than Sendai, but this was augmented in the presence of homologous antiserum as compared with influenza antiserum (solid lines—figure 8-1).

Antiviral immune cytolysis as seen under the microscope using the standard dye exclusion method closely resembles cytolysis with anticell antibody and complement. Cells staining with toluidine blue first appear markedly swollen, then disintegrate leaving cytoplasmic debris and deeply stained nuclei with attached remnants of cytoplasm. These changes precede or accompany the decline in rate of respiration.[8]

The participation of a heat labile factor in rabbit serum was suggested by two observations. When the rabbit antiserum was heated to 56 degrees for twenty minutes cytolysis in the presence of guinea pig complement was greatly reduced. Second, addition of rabbit complement to heated antiserum gave the same or more cytolysis than with guinea pig complement with unheated antiserum.[8] Rabbit complement by itself was slightly more toxic than guinea pig complement at the dilutions used. The possibility that a component inhibitory to guinea pig complement might be formed by heating the rabbit serum was considered, but no evidence for such inhibitor has yet been found by adding an excess of heated normal rabbit serum (practically nontoxic) to the system, unheated antiserum guinea pig complement, and infected cells. Guinea pig

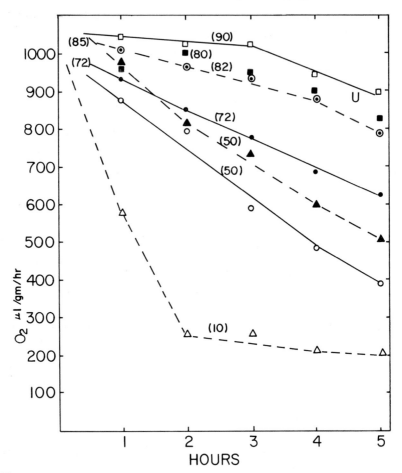

Figure 8-1. Measurement by O_2 consumption of the effect of antiviral anti-body and complement (fresh guinea pig serum 1:20) on cytolysis of murine ascites lymphoma cells infected with Sendai virus. Uninfected cells—☐ no serum or complement. ■ with Sendai antiserum 1:10 and complement. Broken lines, cells infected with 250 HA units/ml Sendai virus: ⊙ PR_8 antiserum 1:10 and complement, △ anti-Sendai serum 1:10 (100 HI units/ml) and complement, ▲ anti-Sendai serum 1:10. Solid lines, cells infected with NDV: 50 HA units/ml. ● PR_8 antiserum 1:10 and complement or no antiserum. O anti-NDV serum 1:10 (25 HI units/ml) and complement. The HI unit was defined as the highest dilution of antiserum which would inhibit hemagglutination by 8 HA units of virus. Numbers in parenthesis indicate percent of cells living as judged by exclusion of toluidine blue at 2.5 hours.

anti-Sendai serum inactivated or not requires the addition of rabbit complement for efficient antiviral immune cytolysis.

The high rate of aerobic glycolysis in most tumor cells facilitates the use of this reaction as a measure of cell viability. In virology changes in the pH of the medium as indicated by the color of phenol red have long been used in tissue culture neutralization tests where killing of cells by virus was demonstrable by relative alkalinity. In the present study cytolysis by antibody and complement has been shown to inhibit glycolysis, and this effect is correlated with inhibition of respiration and changes in membrane permeability as indicated by dye exclusion counts.

To a 1.0 percent suspension of Krebs 2 ascites cells which had been infected eighteen hours previously with Sendai virus was added fresh normal rabbit serum (RaC) and inactivated anti-Sendai immune rabbit serum at a dilution just below the cytolytic end point as determined by dye exclusion. Controls consisted of infected cell suspensions without antiserum, uninfected cell suspensions with RaC and antiserum, and an additional set of these same controls with glucose omitted from the medium. During a five-hour period of incubation the pH was read hourly and again at twenty-four hours.

The results are presented in Figure 8-2. In the controls with glucose the pH dropped after two to three hours to a level of 7.0 - 7.2 where it remained for twenty-four hours. In the tubes containing infected cells, RaC, and antiviral serum the pH remained close to the original level, but showed a decline in the period between five and twenty-four hours. In the presence of higher concentrations of antiserum or RaC the pH remained at 7.6 - 7.8 for twenty-four hours as shown by the broken line at the right. When glucose was omitted from the medium there was no evidence of acid production in the controls except for a slight drop in pH at twenty-four hours which may have been due to accumulation of CO_2 in the closed system. Since glucose in the presence of other substrates does not increase the rate of O_2 uptake of these cells, it is concluded that most of the acid formation was due to glycolysis, not respiratory CO_2. With the ascites lymphoma, in fact, aerobic glycolysis inhibited respiration by 20 to 30 percent (Crabtree effect).

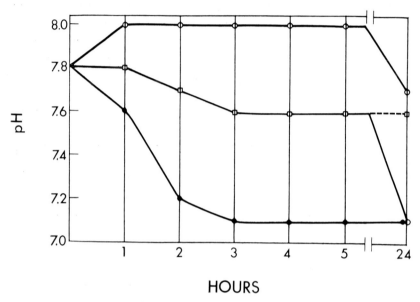

HOURS

Figure 8-2. □ Krebs 2 ascites cells infected with Sendai virus and preincubated eighteen hours. After changing to Eagle's Medium with glocuse, bicarbonate, and one percent bovine albumin, anti-Sendai serum to give final dilutions of 1:80 (8 HAI units/ml) and RaC 1:40 were added and incubation continued. ● Same without antiserum; with uninfected cells curves identical to this were obtained in the presence or absence of antiserum and RaC, O with glucose omitted from medium (no antiserum) controls.

This method, although somewhat less sensitive than dye exclusion and probably not applicable to cells with low aerobic glycolysis, saves much time and labor as a semiquantitative measure of immune cytolysis.

A more convincing model would be presented by the use of syngeneic mouse antiviral serum and cells, preferably with mouse complement. Preliminary experiments, under special conditions, indicate antiviral cytolytic activity of anti-NDV or Sendai antibodies produced in C_3H/Bi mice but with added rabbit complement. Cell destruction is slower and less complete than with rabbit antiviral serum. This may suggest that oncolysis of virus infected cells in virus immune mice as described above may be due to the action of immune lymphocytes rather than antibody and complement, and appropriate models similar to the one described by Dr.

Hotchin are under investigation.

It is also of interest that experiments with immune mice and cell suspensions infected with influenza virus strains instead of the paramyxoviruses NDV and Sendai gave no evidence of antiviral immune cytolysis *in vivo* and only weak antiviral immune cytolysis *in vitro*.[4] This, despite the fact that the respective antisera had comparable hemagglutination inhibition titers, may mean that the influenza group has a different action at the cell membrane although budding as observed by electron microscopy appears very similar to Sendai and NDV. It is also of interest that Sendai or NDV, usually inactivated, are more effective than influenza virus in bringing about cell fusion. We believe that the ascites lymphoma cells used in these studies must be relatively resistant to viral fusion because only occasional clumps of dead cells (by toluidine blue staining) were observed.

These and other similar studies show quite clearly that reaction of viral antigen and antibody at the cell surface will bring about complement dependent cytolysis. When this reaction occurs in the intact animal, especially, in chronic viral infections, the result could simulate autoimmunity and possibly set off a chain of autoimmune reactions in which the host's own tissues become the reactive antigens.

REFERENCES

1. Speel, L.F., Osborn, J.E., and Walker, D.L.: *J Immun, 101*:409, 1968.
2. Holmes, K.V., Klenk, H.D., and Choppin, P.W.: *Proc Soc Exp Biol Med, 131*:651, 1969.
3. Wiktor, T.J., Kuwert, E., and Koprowski, H.: *J Immun, 101*:1271, 1968.
4. Eaton, M.D., and Scala, A.R.: *Proc Soc Exp Biol Med, 132*:20, 1969.
5. Oldstone, M.B.A., and Dixon, F.J.: *J Exp Med., 131*:1, 1970.
6. Chanock, R.M., Parrot, R.H., Kapikian, A.Z., Kim, H.W., and Brandt, C.D.: *Perspect Virol, 6*:125, 1968.
7. Eaton, M.D., Levinthal, J.D., and Scala, A.R.: *J Nat Cancer Inst, 39*:1089, 1967.
8. Eaton, M.D., and Scala, A.R.: *Proc Soc Exp Biol Med, 133*:615, 1970.

Chapter 9

SOME CAUSES AND REPAIR OF ALTERED
ANTIBODY FORMATION IN AGED ANIMALS*

J. WERNER BRAUN

I̲N TERMS of immune responses, aged animals may display two major types of changes: a decline in their capacity to respond to specific antigens and an increased frequency of activation of immune responses to antigen to which they should normally be nonresponsive. The first type of change is quite well documented by experimental data,[1-3] and in some recent studies[4] we demonstrated that it is possible to repair such impaired immunological responsiveness with the aid of chemically defined stimulators that enhance the functions of cells participating in antibody formation. One purpose of this chapter will be a description of these results and a discussion of their possible cellular basis. Then, in an effort to focus attention on possible relationships between changes in hormone-mediated and immunological events in aged individuals, I want to cite some of our recent studies on the enhancement of antibody responses by known mediators of hormone-controlled processes. In addition, I shall consider, on the basis of data collected in studies on the conversion of nonimmunogens into immunogens, possible mechanisms that could account for the development of autoimmune responses in aged individuals. Finally, I want to touch on the problem of nonspecific activation of antibody-forming cell populations as a possible mechanism in the development of autoimmune responses.

*The studies of the author's group herein reviewed have been supported by NIH grant AM-08742, NSF grant B9-0301R, and ACS grant 501. This review was prepared while the author enjoyed the hospitality of the Department of Chemical Immunology, Weizmann Institute (Dr. M. Sela, Head) with the aid of an NIH Special Fellowship.

INFLUENCE OF SYNTHETIC POLYNUCLEOTIDES ON ANTIBODY FORMATION IN AGED MICE

An impairment of antibody formation in old mice has been reported by several investigators.[1-3] We observed[4] in tests with eleven to twelve-month-old $C_{57}B_1$ mice, which represented survivors from a tumor immunity study conducted when the mice were six weeks old, a lack of response (Table 9-I) to sheep red blood cells (sRBC). The responses were assayed with the well-known he-

TABLE 9-I

INFLUENCE OF POLY A + POLY U ON THE RESPONSE TO sRBC IN ELEVEN TO TWELVE-MONTH AND IN SIX-WEEK-OLD FEMALE C57B1 MICE

Treatment of Spleen Donors		$AFC/10^8$ Spleen Cells		
		Day 2	Day 3	Day 4
Old Animals Exp. 1	——	62.7 ± 23.3		
	sRBC (10^8)	95.5 ± 19.2		
	sRBC + AU*	578.7 ± 95.8		
	AU	86.6 ± 67.2		
Old Animals Exp. 2	——	22.8 ± 3.2		
	sRBC (10^8)	38.5 ± 12.5	199.0 ± 63.3	$5,990 \pm 1,277$
	sRBC + AU	386.0 ± 109.7	$3,469.6 \pm 346.5$	$15,578 \pm 4,946$
Young Animals	——	14.4 ± 9.2		
	sRBC (10^8)	75.0 ± 15.2	717.6 ± 162.0	$40,428 \pm 3,541$
	sRBC + AU	459.3 ± 60.3	$4,607.0 \pm 686.0$	$40,501 \pm 6,485$

*150 γ of poly A + 150 γ poly U i.v./mouse. Five animals/group.

molytic plaque technique that measures the number of 19S antibody-forming spleen cells (AFC) in sRBC-immunized animals. As shown in Table 9-I, two separate tests revealed that there was no significant increase in AFC in these old mice (probably more precisely "middle-aged") forty-eight hours after i. v. immunization with 10^8 sRBC, and only little increase after seventy-two hours, above the so-called background number of AFC present in nonimmunized animals. In contrast, young $C_{57}B_1$ animals (see lower part of Table 9-I) normally show an approximately fivefold to eightfold increase above background forty-eight hours after immunization, and an approximately thirtyfold to fiftyfold increase seventy-two hours after immunization. Table 9-I further shows that the simultaneous administration of sRBC and poly A: U, a double-stranded synthetic polynucleotide having one poly A and one poly U strand, resulted in these old animals in a response that exceeded (except for the 4-day group) the normal response obtainable in young animals.

Table 9-II lists comparable results obtained in tests with thirteen-month to fourteen-month-old C57B1 mice that had not been pre-

TABLE 9-II

INFLUENCE OF POLY A + POLY U, POLY G + POLY C, OR POLY I + POLY C ON THE RESPONSE TO sRBC IN OVER THIRTEEN-MONTH-OLD RETIRED C57B1 BREEDERS

Treatment of Spleen Donors	AFC/10^8 Spleen Cells	
	Day 2	Day 3
	41.2 ± 16.5	
sRBC	39.8 ± 12.5	63.3 ± 6.9
sRBC + AU*	328.1 ± 81.5	706.3 ± 30.7
sRBC + GC*	289.7 ± 57.7	741.5 ± 256.8
sRBC + IC*	251.3 ± 36.3	1,206.5 ± 281.8

*150 γ of each of the homopolymers i.v./mouse.

viously employed in other experimental studies. These animals showed an even greater impairment of response to sRBC but, again, the administration of the antigen in conjunction with stimulatory polynucleotides (either poly A + poly U, poly C + poly G, or poly I + poly C) elevated antibody formation, measured in terms of AFC, to levels that surpass nonstimulated responses (i.e. responses to antigen only) of young animals forty-eight hours after immunization, and equalled nonstimulated responses of young animals seventy-two hours after immunization. Additional tests, extended over a period of ten days after immunization (see reference 4), indicated that the poor responsiveness of old C57B1 mice is absolute and does not represent merely a delay in response. Furthermore, tests with old animals from other strains of mice (AKR, CD-1, CF-1) showed that the decline of responses to sRBC is either absent or less pronounced in other strains.

The double-stranded polynucleotides employed in these tests had previously been shown to stimulate, in the presence of antigen, antibody responses in young adult and adult animals,[5-9] to enhance antibody formation *in vitro* (Ishizuka, Webb, and Braun, unpublished data), to initiate premature antibody responses in newborn animals,[10] to produce at least a partial restoration of responses in thymectomized and in irradiated animals,[9] and to enhance cell-mediated immune responses.[12] The stimulatory complex poly A·poly U is known to be nonpyrogenic and apparently lacks significant toxicity, whereas poly I·poly C is pyrogenic and toxic and resembles in many, but not all, properties those of endotoxin.[13] We have discussed elsewhere[13] probable reasons for such differences between nontoxic poly A·poly U and toxic poly I·poly C.

Poly A·poly U is known to have effects on both macrophages and lymphocytes, i.e. the cell types involved in antibody formation. Let us review, with the help of Figure 9-1, some of our present knowledge regarding steps involved in antibody formation. We shall do so in order to pinpoint the various steps at which impairment of antibody formation may occur, even though at present we cannot pinpoint with certainty the step or steps at which the polynucleotide-stimulated repair of antibody formation in aged animals takes place.

It is now generally agreed[14] that the first cell type with which antigen interacts, a cell type that we shall call primary antigen-handling (PAH) cell, may be a member of the macrophage population. An interference with this initial event (see 1, in Fig. 9-1) may therefore impair antibody formation. The precise role of the macrophage-type cells in antibody formation is still not clear; the PAH cells may merely serve to concentrate antigen and to present it to lymphocytes,[15,35] or they may, as proposed in Figure 9-1, process antigen in such a manner that a complex consisting of a pertinent portion of the antigen and a nonspecific activator may result. In any event, the next step is a reaction between the antigenic determinant and an antibody-like receptor site on antigen-reactive lymphocytes. This reaction, either by direct effects resulting from the antigen or by indirect effects resulting from an ability of the antigenic moiety of the antigen-activator complex to 'open up' cells for the 'entrance' of the hypothetical nonspecific activator, will lead to an activation of *potentially* antibody-forming lymphocyte populations. Again, any interference with this event (see 2, in Fig. 9-1) will impair antibody formation. Following appropriate activation of the antigen-reactive stem-cell, a 'silent' multiplication of nonperforming, i.e. of nonantibody-releasing lymphocytes ap-

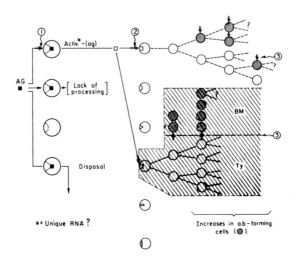

Figure 9-1. Diagrammatic representation of presumed steps in antibody formation. (Recent studies have indicated that events shown in the shaded portion are typical for responses to most antigens. Also, it now appears that carrier-recognition is usually at the level of thymus-dependent cells and hapten-recognition at the level of bone marrow-derived cells. Recognition, if any, at the level of macrophage-like cells appears to be mediated by cytophilic antibody.)

pears to occur.[8, 16-18] The resulting cells, shown as open circles in Figure 9-1, are probably the so-called memory cells, long-lived lymphocytes that after escape from lymphoid organs may possibly become participants in cell-mediated immunity. The nonperforming memory cells in the spleen or lymphnodes apparently can give rise to antibody-forming cells, either by a process of differentiation (upper right hand part of Fig. 9-1) or, according to some recent data of Shearer *et al.*[16] by transmitting a specific signal to other lymphocytes (shaded region of Fig. 9-1). Of pertinence to our considerations here is the recent confirmation,[8, 16, 19] predicted fifteen years ago by Leduc *et al.*,[20] that antigen is required in order to produce the shift from memory cells to antibody-forming cells (see

3, in Fig. 9-1). Thus this represents a third antigen-dependent event which, when altered, may produce an impairment of antibody formation. In addition, any factor depressing the intracellular functions of the two or three cell types involved in antibody formation will depress antibody formation.

As mentioned earlier, poly A:U, and probably also the other stimulatory double-stranded polynucleotides, can enhance the activities of both macrophages and lymphocytes. The effect on macrophages of adult animals has been best documented by Johnson and Johnson[21] who observed a highly significant stimulation of antibody responses to BGG following a relatively brief period of *in vitro* exposure of peritoneal macrophages to poly A:U, followed by an injection of treated macrophages and antigen into syngeneic mice. Winchurch and Braun (unpublished data) have observed that a stimulation of the rate of clearance of staphylococci from the peritoneal cavity of mice occurs within forty-five to sixty minutes after i.p. administration of poly A:U. In addition, it was demonstrated that a premature initiation of antibody formation in newborn mice which can be elicited by a transfer of syngeneic adult macrophages into newborns[22,23] can also be produced without cell transfer, namely by the administration of polynucleotides to newborns, a treatment that presumably leads to a stimulation of the recipients' immature macrophages.[10] Stimulatory effects of polynucleotides on macrophages also have been observed in some of our recent studies on antibody formation by spleen cell population *in vitro* (Ishizuka, Webb, and Braun, unpublished data).*

As far as effects of polynucleotides on lymphocytes are concerned, a striking enhancement of the early rate of increase in antibody-forming spleen cell populations, following the administration of antigen with synthetic double-stranded polynucleotides, was observed by us quite some time ago,[5] at a time when the role of multiplying precursor cells had not yet been recognized and when, in the absence of such knowledge, the effect was ascribed solely to an increased rate of multiplication of antibody-forming cells.[5] It now appears more likely that apart from possible effects on the multiplication of antibody-forming cells, a stimulation of the rate

---

*It should be noted that, in contrast to *in vivo* systems, enhancing effects *in vitro* are produced principally by single-stranded polynucleotides.

of multiplication of memory cells and an enhancement of the occurrence of the shift from memory cells to antibody-forming cells (see 3, in Fig. 9-1) may be involved. A stimulation of the rate of increase in memory cell populations is suggested by preliminary data,[24] the influence of poly A:U on the shift from memory cells to antibody-forming cells has been observed in experimental studies that have been reported elsewhere.[8] Finally, to judge by the ability of polynucleotides to enhance circulating antibody titers during postimmunization periods when there is little or no further increase in the number of antibody-forming cells,[12] they must also be able to stimulate the performance of individual antibody-forming cells.

Lack of availability of aged animals has prevented us so far from determining at which of these various modifiable steps in antibody synthesis polynucleotides may exert their restorative effects on impaired antibody formation in aged animals. However, attempts to fill this gap in our knowledge by appropriate experimentation are under way. Prior data by Albright and Makinodan[2] have suggested that the functions of both macrophages and lymphocytes may be impaired in old animals.

Concerning the mode of action of polynucleotides on macrophages and lymphocytes, it appears that the undegraded polyanion can exert an effect on macrophage membranes, whereas oligomers, derived from the polynucleotides by depolymerization *in vivo*, may stimulate lymphocyte-associated events.[13]

Before we leave the polynucleotides, one more point must be mentioned. It is now known that ordinarily poorly immunogenic or nonimmunogenic materials, e.g., syngeneic tumor cells,[12,25-26] can become good immunogens when administered together with synthetic polynucleotides. Apparently, the latter enhance the responsiveness of the host sufficiently to permit a response to otherwise ineffective antigens. We have known for quite a long time that naturally occurring breakdown products of nucleic acids can produce similar stimulatory effects,[27] that such materials can be released by cell injury,[28] and that very young animals can be stimulated by polynucleotides, above their normal response, to a greater extent than older animals.[29] It is therefore possible that while some old animals, like the old C57B1 mice that we discussed earlier, lack responsiveness and are restimulated by artificially administered polynucleotides, other old animals, particularly after prolonged periods of tissue damage, might have naturally high extracellular levels of stimulatory nucleic acids and may therefore respond to materials that are ordinarily not immunogenic (or that are ordinarily present in concentration insufficient for evoking a response). One wonders whether such a condition may exist, for example, in NZB mice that are known to produce autoimmune responses; the recent finding that such animals produce antibodies to nucleic acids following the administration of poly I'poly C[30] may, perhaps, reflect such heightened responses to naturally present materials as a result of an excess of stimulators, if it should turn out that the observed responses are not merely due to a capacity of poly I'poly C itself to be immunogenic in such animals.

INFLUENCE OF CYCLIC AMP AND Ca⁺⁺ LEVELS ON ANTIBODY FORMATION

A possible clue regarding the manner in which stimulatory polynucleotides may affect cells involved in antibody formation has come from recent observations on the capacity of cyclic AMP, a known mediator of intracellular events in hormone-controlled activations,[31] to enhance antibody formation.[32] Data summarized in Table 9-III show that cyclic AMP enhances the early rate of appearance of AFC in sRBC-immunized animals and, furthermore, that theophylline, a known stablizer of cyclic AMP, potentiates poly A:U effects, leading to stimulated responses even in the presence of otherwise insufficient concentrations of poly A:U. Studies on hormone-elicited cellular activations have shown that reactions between a specific hormone and a specific membrane-associated receptor site lead to the activation of a membrane-associated enzyme, adenyl cyclase, which converts ATP into cyclic AMP, the latter activating, in turn, kinases that control the formation or activity of enzymes.[31] In view of the demonstration that cyclic AMP can modify antibody formation, and that a stabilizer of cyclic AMP can potentiate poly A:U effects, it is tempting to assume that interactions between a specific antigen and receptor sites on immunocompetent cells may trigger intracellular events in a fashion quite similar to those encountered in hormone-controlled activations and that poly A'poly U may enhance these particular events.

TABLE 9-III

THE EFFECTS OF cAMP (200 γ / MOUSE I.P.), DB-cAMP (VARIOUS
DOSES I.V.), AND THEOPHYLLINE (200 γ / MOUSE I.P.) ON
ANTIBODY FORMATION TO SHEEP RED BLOOD
CELLS IN CFW MICE

The mice were tested in the absence and presence of concomitant i.v. administration of poly A:U. The effects of cAMP were also tested after simultaneous administration of ALS (0.1 ml/mouse i.p.). There were five animals per group. Assays were made by determining the number of antibody-forming spleen cells by the hemolytic plaque technique.

Treatment of Spleen Donors	Average Number (± S.E.) of AFC per 10^8 Nucleated Spleen Cells After 48 Hrs.
A. Unimmunized controls	61.1 ± 10.4
sRBC (10^8)	642.3 ± 75.0
sRBC (10^8) + cAMP	1,303.2 ± 284.9
sRBC (10^8) + cAMP + ALS	3,027.5 ± 238.6
sRBC (10^8) + ALS	487.4 ± 124.6
sRBC (10^8) + poly A:U	5,904.7 ± 475.8
sRBC (10^8) + poly A:U + cAMP	4,040.6 ± 705.7
B. Unimmunized controls	69.0 ± 10.4
sRBC(10^8)	613.9 ± 65.7
sRBC (10^8) + DB-cAMP (500 γ)	1,342.8 ± 154.2
sRBC (10^8) + DB-cAMP (1,000 γ)	1,666.2 ± 85.5
——————— DB-cAMP (1,000 γ)	42.0 ± 9.1
C. Unimmunized controls	36.6 ± 3.0
sRBC (10^8)	299.2 ± 42.4
sRBC (10^8) + poly A:U (300 γ)	1,743.5 ± 70.4
sRBC (10^8) + poly A:U (300 γ) + theophylline	2,635.8 ± 138.3
sRBC (10^8) + theophylline	277.5 ± 114.4
D. Unimmunized controls	30.3 ± 4.6
sRBC (10^8)	493.1 ± 46.7
sRBC (10^8) + poly A:U (3 γ)	346.8 ± 38.9
sRBC (10^8) + poly A:U (3γ) + theophylline	707.0 ± 55.7
sRBC (10^8) + poly A:U (30 γ)	1,428.9 ± 260.3
sRBC (10^8) + poly A:U(30γ) + theophylline	1,889.8 ± 151.0
sRBC (10^8) + poly A:U (300 γ)	1,757.0 ± 267.5
sRBC (10^8) + poly A:U (300 γ) + theophylline	3,230.7 ± 208.7

Thus parallels may exist between age-dependent changes in hormone-elicited and antigen-elicited events.

Studies with endocrine systems also have demonstrated that elevated Ca^{++} levels may stimulate events leading to the activation of cyclic AMP.[33] Similarly, we have recently found that antibody formation can either be enhanced or suppressed by an elevation of Ca^{++} levels *in vivo*[34] or *in vitro* systems (Ishizuka and Braun, unpublished data). The direction of the change, whether enhancement or suppression, is dependent on the time of alteration of Ca^{++} levels in relation to the time of administration of antigen.[34] Since Ca^{++} is known to affect a large variety of membrane-associated events,[34] these observations may serve as further evidence for the critical role of membrane-associated events in the activation of immune responses and they emphasize the likelihood that many age-dependent changes may be due to altered membrane structures or functions.

CONVERSION OF NONIMMUNOGENS INTO IMMUNOGENS BY BASIC PROTEINS AND OTHER CARRIERS

A third aspect that I wish to consider is the possibility that some autoimmune responses in aging animals may occur as a consequence of possible age-dependent accumulations of serum factors that can convert ordinarily nonimmunogenic materials into potent immunogens. My considerations are based on the now very well known role of so-called carriers in antibody formation[35-36] and on the knowledge that the use of foreign proteins, specifically of basic proteins, as carriers can convert many nonimmunogens or weak immunogens into good immunogens.[37] It is well established that a number of simple organic substances, as well as certain complex molecules, which by themselves fail to initiate antibody production, and which are termed *haptens*, will elicit responses when coupled to certain proteins.[35] The general assumption is that haptens fail to interact with PAH cells or other immunocompetent cells participating in antibody formation, but will be channeled into immunologically responsive cell systems when they are associated with an easily recognized carrier, part of which then may or may not contribute to the antigenic specificity of the hapten to which the carrier is coupled.[35] There is, in addition, another mechanism that may be held responsible for the immunogenicity of certain protein-conjugated or protein-complexed materials that ordinarily fail to elicit immune responses, and that is a carrier-elicited protection of haptenic polymers against depolymerization by enzymes present in the animal. Thus, a potential immunogen that is rapidly depoly-merized in the body and is thereby rendered nonimmunogenic may produce immune responses when coupled to a material that pro-tects it against enzymatic attack. A pertinent example that may combine both of these carrier-associated features is the potential immunogenicity of nucleic acids. These substances, injected either as oligonucleotides or polynucleotides into an animal fail to evoke antibody formation, but will readily do so when conjugated co-valently to a foreign protein or when complexed electrostatically to a basic foreign protein.[38] Thus, immunization with a complex of (basic) methylated bovine serum albumin (MBSA) and (acidic) heterologous or homologous nucleic acids results in the formation of antibodies specific for the nucleic acid moiety of the immuno-gen.[37-38] Similarly, certain ordinarily nonimmunogenic polysac-charides (e.g., purified pneumococcal polysaccharide in rabbits) and polypeptides (e.g., poly-L-glutamic acid) can be rendered im-munogenic by complexing, through mere mixing, with MBSA.[37] Moreover, an animal's own tissue can be rendered immunogenic by complexing with basic proteins. Thus, Plescia has shown that rab-bit heart or kidney tissue complexed with MBSA becomes im-munogenic in rabbits.[35] In studies with syngeneic tumor cells, in-spired by such results, we have demonstrated that the exposure of chemically or virus-induced tumor cells to basic foreign protein (we used methylated bovine gamma globulin in experiments with mice) will result in immune responses that are not obtainable with non-complexed tumor cells (Braun and Plescia, unpublished data). Extrapolating from such results to possible mechanisms of develop-ment of autoimmune responses, it may be suggested that the accum-ulation of degraded basic proteins within an individual, as a possible consequence of tissue destruction, may lead to the development of immunogenic complexes containing basic proteins plus acidic con-stitutents of self-antigens. Closely related considerations have been discussed in more detail by Nastuk and Plescia.[38a]

We already mentioned the recent observation of Steinberg *et al.*[30] that NZB mice produce antibodies to nucleic acids following the administration of ordinarily nonimmunogenic poly I-poly C. This may well reflect the presence of a factor, perhaps an unnatural basic protein, in such animals, capable of complexing with the polynucleotide and rendering it immunogenic. It would be interesting to know whether treatment of polynucleotides with sera from NZB mice would render these materials immunogenic for other strains of mice.

Perhaps even more pertinent to the type of consideration that we have discussed here is the finding[35, 38b] that sensitization of a host to a hapten (e.g., to DNP as a consequence of immunization of rabbits with BSA-DNP) permits subsequent responses to ordinarily nonimmunogenic materials to which the hapten has been attached (e.g., DNP-conjugates of homologous tissue antigens). Thus it can be anticipated that an animal naturally sensitized to a foreign antigen may subsequently develop autoimmune responses when the same foreign antigen happens to combine in an appropriate manner with a normal tissue component of the animal.

'NONSPECIFIC' ACTIVATION OF ANTIBODY-FORMING CELL POPULATIONS AND ITS POSSIBLE RELATIONSHIP TO AUTOIMMUNE PHENOMENA

A substantial body of evidence indicates that one and the same lymphocyte population capable of potential synthesis of a given immunoglobulin can either be triggered to nonresponsiveness or to antibody formation.[14] In other words, the precursor of antibody-forming cell populations and the tolerant cell are identical. A number of theories have been advanced to explain this situation. For example, Bretscher and Cohn[39] have suggested that one signal, acting on the membrane, may be required to induce tolerance whereas two signals may be needed to induce antibody formation. We have suggested an alternative mechanism, namely that a complex of nonspecific activator and antigen, interacting with the appropriate antibody-like receptor on the ARC (see 2, in Fig. 9-1) activates precursors of antibody-forming cell populations, whereas an interaction between ARC and 'naked' antigen, i.e. antigen devoid of activator because of a lack of processing by PAH cells, will lead to nonresponsiveness. Such nonresponsiveness should be specific and lasting since the interaction between the specific receptor site(s) on the ARC and 'naked' antigen, while activating nothing, will produce a 'clogging' of the receptor site that would be needed for any subsequent activation. Activation of 'clogged' cells could only occur if the hypothetical activator could enter, or interact with, 'clogged' cells via sites other than the receptor site. The impairment of functions of the PAH cells, which in our scheme produce the complex of activator and antigen, would be expected to lead to a specific and lasting nonresponsiveness to antigens that are presented at the time of such impairment. The literature contains a number of examples indicating that this is the case in adult animals [8, 40-41] and apparently also in the early stages of development of an animal.[10] Furthermore, we have supplied experimental data[8] that show that whenever a specific antigen is administered together with a modifier of lymphocyte membranes (e.g., with antilymphocyte serum, epinephrine, chlorpromazine, or streptolysine) a *specific* response is converted into a weak but significant *nonspecific* response. An example of such an effect is shown in Table 9-IV which

TABLE 9-IV

INFLUENCE OF EPINEPHRINE ON THE SPECIFICITY OF THE
ANTIBODY RESPONSE TO KEYHOLE LIMPET HEMOCYANIN (KLH)

Treatment of Spleen Donors	Average Number ($\pm$ S.E.) of Hemolysin-producing Cells per 10^8 Nucleated Spleen Cells after 48 Hours Assayed on	
	sRBC*	hRBC*
None	18.5 $\pm$ 1.7	12.4 $\pm$ 1.9
KLH (10 γ/mouse)	27.5 $\pm$ 3.6†	26.7 $\pm$ 2.3‡
KLH + epinephrine	70.0 $\pm$ 14.9†	93.4 $\pm$ 12.8‡
Epinephrine	19.5 $\pm$ 2.7	20.4 $\pm$ 9.8

*sRBC=sheep red blood cells; hRBC=horse red blood cells.
†0.02 < P < 0.05.
‡P < 0.01.

illustrates that whereas immunization of mice with keyhole limpet hemocyanin will ordinarily lead to little activation beyond the normal background of spleen cells forming antibodies to sRBC, administration of this antigen together with epinephrine will produce significant increases in antibody-forming cells producing anti-sRBC. We have interpreted such results as a consequence of a general effect on lymphocyte membranes that may lead to an abrogation of the guidance functions of the antigen. In other words, and in somewhat naive terms, while antigen normally would serve to 'open up' only appropriate cells (i.e. with the proper antibody-like receptor site) for the entrance of the nonspecific activator, a change in permeability of all lymphocytic ARC because of an agent such as epinephrine, may open up numerous inappropriate cells for the entrance of the activator. The consequence is a nonspecific weak response (due to lack of the specific driving antigen at step 3 in Fig. 9-1) rather than a strong specific response. Whatever the ultimate explanation for this phenomenon might be, what is of pertinence to our consideration here is the fact that agents affecting membrane structure and functions can convert specific antibody responses into weak nonspecific responses, and this raises the possibility that such membrane changes might occur normally as a consequence of aging and may result in the production of ineffective nonspecific responses rather than strong specific responses. We have made some limited observations with old mice that have suggested that the specificity of the antibody response may be reduced with age. So far such results have been too meager to justify documentation, but they are cited to encourage further studies along these lines.

In summary, experiments with aged mice have shown that poor antibody responses can be restored to normal or even above normal responses with the aid of stimulatory synthetic polynucleotides which are known to enhance the functions of macrophages and lymphocytes. Studies with modifiers of immunological and hormone-mediated events have supported the concept that membrane-associated events are critical for the initiation and regulation of immune responses, and thus, changes in membranes may be one of the factors responsible for altered immune responses in the aged. Finally, we have noted the possibility that autoimmune responses may develop in old animals as a consequence of a natural accumulation of substances converting nonimmunogens into immunogens, as a result of an accumulation of natural stimulators of immune responses, and possibly also as a result of a breakdown of the mechanisms that lead ordinarily to the activation of appropriate and specific preexisting stem-cells of antibody-forming cell populations.

REFERENCES

1. Makinodan, T., and Peterson, W.J.: *J Immun, 93*:886, 1964.
2. Albright, J.F., and Makinodan, T.: *J Cell Physiol, 67 (Suppl. 1)*:185, 1966.
3. Metcalf, D., Moulds, R., and Pike, B.: *Clin Exp Immun, 2*:109, 1967.
4. Braun, W., Yajima, Y., and Ishizuka, M.: *J RES, 7*:418, 1970.
5. Braun, W., and Nakano, M.: *Science, 157*:819, 1967.
6. Braun, W., and Firshein, W.: *Bact Rev, 31*:83, 1967.
7. Braun, W., Nakano, M., Jaraskova, L., Yajima, Y., and Jimenez, L.: In Plescia, O.J., and Braun, W. (Eds): *Nucleic Acids in Immunology.* New York, Springer-Verlag, 1968, p. 347.
8. Braun, W., Yajima, Y., Jimenez, L., and Winchurch, R.: In Sterzl, J. (Ed.): *Developmental Aspects of Antibody Formation and Structure.* New York, Academic Press, 1970.
9. Johnson, A.: In Sterzl, J. (Ed.): *Developmental Aspects of Antibody Formation and Structure.* New York, Academic Press, 1970.
10. Winchurch, R., and Braun, W.: *Nature, 223*:843, 1969.
11. Jaroslow, B.N.: In Plescia, O.J., and Braun, W. (Eds.): *Nucleic Acids in Immunology.* New York, Springer-Verlag, 1968, p. 404.
12. Braun, W.: *Proceedings of the VIth International Congress of Chemotherapy.* Tokyo, 1970.
13. Braun, W.: *Nature, 224*:1024, 1969.
14. Landy, M., and Braun, W.: *Immunological Tolerance: A reassessment of mechanisms of antibody formation.* New York, Academic Press, 1969.
15. Askonas, B.: In Sterzl, J. (Ed.): *Developmental Aspects of Antibody Formation and Structure.* New York, Academic Press, 1970.
16. Shearer, G.M., and Cudkowicz, G.: *J Exp Med, 130*:1243, 1969.
17. Mitchell, G.F., and Miller, J.F.A.P.: *J Exp Med, 128*:821, 1968.
18. Perkins, E.H., Sado, T., and Makinodan, T.: *J Immun, 103*:668, 1969.
19. Graf, M.W., and Uhr, J.W.: *J Exp Med, 130*:1175, 1969.
20. Leduc, E.H., Coons, A.H., and Connolly, J.M.: *J Exp Med, 102*:61, 1955.
21. Johnson, H.G., and Johnson, A.G.: *Bact Proc*, p. 99, 1969.
22. Braun, W., and Lasky, L.J.: *Fed Proc, 26*:642, 1967.
23. Argyris, B.F.: *J Exp Med, 128*:459, 1968.
24. Jimenez, L.: *Studies on the Initiation and Regulation of Antibody Formation to Sheep Red Blood Cells in Mice.* Thesis, Rutgers University, 1969.
25. Levy, H.B., Law, L.W., and Rabson, A.S.: *Proc Nat Acad Sci, 62*:357, 1969.
26. Larson, V.M., Clark, W.R., and Hilleman, M.R.: *Proc Soc Exp Biol Med, 131*:1002, 1969.
27. Braun, W., and Nakano, M.: *Proc Soc Exp Biol Med, 119*:701, 1965.
28. Nakano, M., and Braun, W.: *J Immunol, 99*:570, 1967.
29. Hechtel, M., Dishon, T., and Braun, W.: *Proc Soc Exp Biol Med, 120*:728, 1965.

30. Steinberg, A.D., Baron, S., and Talal, N.: *Proc Nat Acad Sci, 63*:1102, 1969.
31. Robison, G.A., Butcher, R.W., and Sutherland, E.W.: *Ann Rev Biochem, 37*:149, 1968.
32. Ishizuka, M., Gafni, M., and Braun, W.: *Proc Soc Exp Biol Med, 134*: 963, 1970.
33. Whitfield, J.F., Perris, A.D., and Youdale, T.: *J Cell Physiol, 73*:203, 1968.
34. Braun W., Ishizuka, M., and Seeman, P.: *Nature, 226*:945, 1970.
35. Plescia, O.: *Curr Top Microbiol Immun, 50*:78, 1969.
36. Sela, M.: *Science, 166*:1365, 1969.
37. Plescia, O.J., and Braun, W.: *Advances Immun, 6*:231, 1967.
38. Plescia, O.J., and Braun, W.: *Nucleic Acids in Immunology.* New York, Springer-Verlag, 1968.
38a. Nastuk, W.L., and Plescia, O.J.: *Ann NY Acad Sci, 135*:664, 1966.
38b. Plescia, O.J., Nastuk, W.L., and Johnson, V.: In Rose, N.R., and Milgrom, F. (Eds.): *International Convocation on Immunology.* Basel, New York, S. Karger, 1969.
39. Bretscher, P.A., and Cohn, M.: *Nature, 220*:444, 1968.
40. Feldman, M., and Gallily, R.: *Cold Spring Harbor Symposium, Quantitative Biology, 32*:415, 1967.
41. Sabet, T.Y., and Friedman, H.: *Proc Soc Biol Med, 131*:1317, 1969.